MW00931344

"Matt's story of redemption, love and commitment to God is one of the better stories I've ever heard in college baseball. As illustrated in this book, Matt is a true testament that when there is a will, there is a way, both on and off the field. His story resonates with many in our sport, and even more in the game of life."
-Kendall Rogers
Managing Editor, D1Baseball.com

"I have known Matt for over 40 years and in that time I have watched him grow as a man and overcome tremendous obstacles. I could not be more proud of what he has accomplished in his career. He is a tremendous husband, father, and developer of young men. Most importantly, he lives his faith every day with uncompromising principles and does not waver to the pressures and temptations of his job. To Matt, first and foremost, it is always about developing young ball players into men. In our *win now and at all cost* culture in sports, that is a very unique and special quality to have as a coach. He is developing men to be better husbands, fathers and productive members of our communities. Furthermore, he is developing future leaders who can carry on his values to others."
-Chris Ballard
General Manager, Indianapolis Colts

"The true measure of success is the impact you have on the people you encounter through life. Matt has the ability to dig deep in your soul and bring the best out of the people who are willing to listen. I would stop and take a minute to read his message; it has helped me become a better person and leader."

-Duke Austin
President, Quanta Services

"15 to 28 is a wonderful story of perseverance and the ability to overcome adversity. Matt is a great baseball man and one of the greatest team builders I have ever known. He is also one of my best friends and has been for the last twenty-five years. From the peaks of the greatest mountains to the deepest and darkest valleys, God always puts people in our lives to help us overcome anything. The darkness that overcame Matt's life and his story only has a happy ending because of the many 'God Winks' along his path. Matt has always been surrounded by great witness, although many times it was hard to see. In Matt's journey it isn't hard to see that Coach Robichaux saved his baseball life but quite possibly, just by providing opportunity and wisdom, saved a lot more than a baseball career. Matt's wife Kathy is the true unsung hero in this entire story. Kathy is the rock and the glue that kept a family going and kept a marriage going that in the end kept a man going. Again, God always surrounds us with everything and everyone that we need for all seasons of our lives. We just have to be humble enough to see the winks!!!!"

-Rob Childress
Head Coach Baseball Coach, Texas A&M University

15 TO 28

A STORY OF GOD'S LOVE, POWER AND REDEMPTION

COACH MATT DEGGS

15 to 28
A Story of God's Love, Power, and Redemption

Copyright © 2018 by Matt Deggs

ISBN-13: 978-1981338917
ISBN-10: 1981338918

To learn more about Coach Matt Deggs, visit
CoachDeggs.com

TABLE OF CONTENTS

Foreword

It is an honor and a privilege to write this foreword for someone I greatly respect. Matt's raw and honest story comes straight from his heart. I truly believe God puts our work in our heart and connects our feet to our heart. When our heart is not fully engaged, our feet take us out. Matt's journey is a great story in redemption to not only save himself but his family.

When Matt and I met in a hotel for hours, I never asked him what had happened at Texas A&M. I have never cared about what a man has done; what I really want to know is what is he going to do about it? We always have to remember that no matter what we are drowning in, our lifeguard, Jesus Christ, once walked on water. Addiction of any kind is a temporary solution to a permanent problem. Finding Christ is a permanent solution to a temporary problem. Matt found the greatest doctor there is to heal his brokenness, "Jesus Christ." The Church is not a Hall of Fame for the perfect; it's a hospital for the broken.

Most people think I hired Matt that day because he is a great hitting coach. I hired Matt that day because I saw a man who was broken and needed healing. I also saw in his eyes and heart that he was not only trying to heal himself but that his number one priority was to not lose his wife and three children just to be a successful baseball coach. As a coach, God doesn't want our success; He wants our surrender. I saw a man that wanted to be a "Godly" Father, not just a father; there is a big difference. In life the devil wants us to believe that what we did when we fell becomes who we are. Sin is what we did; it doesn't have to become who we are. The devil wanted him to take his mess and live in it. Matt did what

Christ wants us to do; that is, to take our **mess** and make it our **message** and to take our **test** and make it our **testament**.

I respect Matt for having the courage to share his story. We have to stop worrying about who we are going to offend in this country and start worrying about who we are going to inspire. It was a great honor to mentor and coach alongside Matt Deggs. In this book he will give me some credit for helping him, but truth be told, he helped me. Our relationship will always be strong because what I needed Matt provided and what Matt needed I provided. There is no way you can read this book and not be changed. You get to read it; I got the opportunity to live it, and for that I will always be blessed.

A good coach makes a boy a better baseball player, but a great coach makes a boy a better man – Matt Deggs is a Great Coach.

-Tony Robichaux
Head Baseball Coach, University of Louisiana at Lafayette

Dedication

There is a song by the David Crowder Band called "Never Let Go." I now listen to that song before every game and have since 2014. This book is dedicated to those of you, and you know who you are, that "never let go." I love you with all my heart and will never forget!

To my many brothers and sisters out there living in despair, guilt, shame, lost, broken, alone, and hopeless. There is a better way, I promise you. In the book of Luke, Jesus says that the healthy don't need a doctor. No...He came to heal the sick. It is my hope that this story would be medicine for your soul!

Chapter 1
The 2nd Summit

"We made it to the second summit. We made history, but we didn't get to plant our flag."
~ Coach Matt Deggs, speaking on his Sam Houston State University Bearkat baseball team's history-making run at the conclusion of the 2017 season

Story #1

The Press Conference

June 11, 2017

"This is a family. You know, for years I was a transactional coach. What can I get? What can I get? And uh, when you get fired, it humbles you. I spent 430 days outside the game. Everybody asked, *Uh, you know you were here with the Aggies in 2011.* No, I wasn't. I was fired, and, uh, I had to sit there and watch the Aggies play. God has brought me full circle and changed my life. I was dead, and He saved me. And… so I'm a transformational coach now. It's not about wins or losses. It's about love. It's about building men. It's about building relationships that will last forever. I got a second chance. This guy is a second-chance guy. This guy is a second-chance guy. This guy is a second-chance guy. We are about building people up. You know, it's not 'mission Omaha.' It's 'mission build and save lives,' and that's what we are in the business of doing. This is the most unselfish, selfless group of men and families that I have ever been around. This is rare in this day and age. Rare in a microwave society where it's all about entitlement and all about 'when do

I get to play.' This guy is playing with a broken left hand right now. Nobody knows that his left hand is broken. Last year he played with a broken wrist. Last year Taylor Beene played with a broken thumb. I won't even get into the rest of the litany of injuries that is going on with this team right now. Andrew Fregia just walked up to me in the dugout and said, 'Give my last at-bat to Nate VanDyke.' Robie Rojas gave up his last at-bat so Hunter Southerland could catch. You know, there is no greater honor, and, uh this is...I could preach. This is what I wish our country would get back to. There is no greater honor than to sacrifice for a brother, and that encapsulates and embodies this team to a tee... That's why they're so lovable."

With those 350 words that led to 40 million plus views of the video of that press conference, my life changed forever. When I was leaving the University of Louisiana Ragin' Cajuns in the summer of 2014, God spoke to my heart after the final team meeting with my hitters: "I am going to take you and put you on just a little bigger stage." We had just finished a historical season, so immediately my mind went to, "Awesome! I'm going to get a big job at a huge school." Looking back now, little did I know He had a different stage in mind, like a table in a meeting room at Florida State after enduring a 19-0 whooping, surrounded by cameras, support staff, players, and microphones. The Lord's ways truly are higher than ours, and His thoughts much higher too. I can honestly say that if I met you on the street today and you asked me to repeat that press conference, I would not even come close. To this day I still have no idea what I said. That press conference was a message from the Holy Spirit, and the words were simply spoken through me.

The morning of that final game in Tallahassee, I woke up early like I always do, especially on game days. Kathy was still in bed asleep in our hotel room. I was trying to be quiet while I was going through my daily devotional at the desk next to our bed. I don't remember the topic of the devotional that morning, but I do distinctly remember the Lord speaking into my heart, "Tell your story!" If you have ever encountered a moment when the Holy Spirit nudges you, then you know it's undeniable and unmistakable! Still being selfish in my ways, my first thought was, "Oh my goodness, we are going to come back and win this whole thing!" I actually responded to the Lord in my mind with, "I promise I will tell the story. I will tell the entire story as soon as we get to Omaha... I will tell the entire thing, Lord!" You see, just the day before, my Sam Houston State University Bearkats and the Southland Conference which we compete in had found itself in "rarified air" – competing at Florida State University against the Seminoles in our school and the conference's first-ever Super Regional.* Just a week earlier we had gone to Lubbock, Texas, and pulled off the seemingly impossible by taking down two of the top teams in the country – the Arizona Wildcats and the host team, Texas Tech Red Raiders. We had a 3-run lead in that first game at FSU in the 7th inning with two outs, no one on base and "Big D" (Dakota Mills) on the mound. We had sucked the Seminoles into the exact game that we had played all year by spinning the game out of control offensively. We had gotten to All-American starter Tyler Holton, our pitchers had pounded the strike zone, and we had dominated routine plays defensively, even turning a triple play at one point! Needless to say, everyone in our dugout "knew" we were going to win that first game, but FSU responded and did something I have never seen before. With two outs in the 7th, their leadoff man reached on a perfectly executed drag bunt, and then they followed that with four straight 2-out line-drive singles up the middle to tie the game. FSU would eventually walk us off in the bottom of the 9th and win that first game 7-6. Obviously, we were all disappointed, but this ball club was very resilient. They had incredibly short memories, still expected to come back, win two straight games, and advance to Omaha.** We were all very confident. That's why, when the Lord nudged me to tell my story, my automatic assumption was, "YES! Lord, you are going to bless us to come back and win this entire thing!" Very selfish, immature thinking and logic, I know, but that person still lives inside of me. Therefore, I have to make a focused effort each day to humble myself.

All set to tell "my story" after we came back and won this super regional, we loaded up, got to the ballpark at FSU, and got ready for the second game. We had our All-American ace, Heath Donica, on the mound, and everyone expected to come out and win. We had no doubt! However, the good Lord had other plans for me, our coaches, and this unforgettable group of grinders that He had blessed us to coach. It went down like this: A game that was supposed to start at 12 o'clock noon ultimately didn't begin until close to 8:00 pm. An All-American pitcher that is accustomed to a very meticulous routine was forced to change this routine three separate times. Then a team with a mountain of expectation finally succumbed to the rigors of adversity, disappointment, and setback. FSU, being the great team that they are, at home and holding a 1-0 lead in the series, smelled blood in the water, and took advantage of every opportunity. Our kids, competing like the warriors that they are, would not quit. Like a prized fighter in the 15th round of a heavyweight bout, FSU was going to have to knock them out. For me personally, I have never been a guy that can let go either. That can be a double-edged sword, but when the score hit 14-0, I called up the boys and told them it was okay. "Have fun, enjoy this time, love your brothers, and play like you don't know what the score is," and with that I effectively threw in the towel because I could not bear to see these boys go out on the canvas. For the remaining three innings, we laughed, we loved, we forgot the score, and we enjoyed our final moments together. On a personal note, the light bulb had finally gone off for me. God didn't want my story in Omaha. He wanted my story now, amid the largest defeat in school history.

* A super regional is the best 2-3 series that takes place to determine the eight teams that will compete in Omaha.
**Omaha is the host city for the College World Series.

Monday, June 12, 2017 – I had such high hopes for this day. This was going to be the day that we punched our ticket to Omaha, Nebraska, the crown jewel of college baseball and every team's end goal. This was playing on loop in my mind as I was eating breakfast at our hotel with the coaches, players, and families. That morning I had several conversations with people whom I loved and cared about, but honestly, I had no clue what they were saying, as I was lost in my own remorse, dealing with the disappointment that comes from getting so close to your destination but then having to turn around. Little did I know that the "winds of change" were swirling around me. Something I never could have imagined was on the horizon. As we boarded the plane to leave Tallahassee (yes, it was still raining), several players began gathering around asking if I was aware that last night's press conference was going "viral." My first response was, "What is viral?" Then I thought to myself, "Oh my goodness, 'viral'?" They assured me it was not bad, but only that it meant our message was being shared rapidly across the internet in very high volume. I am NOT a tech guy. At the time, I did not even have a Twitter account. High tech for me is the GroupMe app that we use to communicate with the team.

We boarded the plane, buckled in, said goodbye to Tallahassee, and headed back to Huntsville. I knew it was going to be a long afternoon. As my thoughts raced during the two-hour flight from Florida to Texas, I was going back and forth in my mind on what to say. You see, this would be the last time that this team would ever be together. Since we are a program that values efficiency, we were going to put the 2017 season to bed in one day. That meant that we would have our final team meeting, meet with everybody individually, and say our goodbyes. The way that my mind works is, "Tomorrow we start the 2018 season, and time is of the essence." There is zero rest time in college baseball. The day you decide to take a break, somebody is outworking you. Consequently, that is exactly what happens when you play this late into the postseason. You find yourself feeling behind and chasing your tail in the recruiting game.

I knew this last team meeting would be difficult, and I honestly didn't think it would come for another couple of weeks. I didn't really have the words for these guys. It wasn't until we arrived back on campus and walked into the clubhouse that it came to me. Apparently, during the two-hour flight, "the video" really began to go viral. The boys were going nuts, coming up to me, showing me names like Kurt Warner, Kirk Herbstreit, and Zach Johnson to name a few. At that instant, I realized what we were in this for. I gathered the boys in the meeting room, grabbed a bottle of water, took a huge gulp, and made my way to the podium. "Boys, do you see this bottle?" I asked. "Yes," they replied. "Boys, do you know what's in this bottle?" One of them said, "Yeah, it's water, Coach." I asked them to tell me about water, to which someone replied, "We drink it." I said, "Somebody else tell me about water?" Another replied, "We need it." Then I cut to the heart of the matter. "Can water save your life?" Every single one of them answered with a resounding, "Yes!" Shifting gears, I then asked, "What is carrying this water?" A bunch of guys muttered out, "plastic" or "a bottle." Finally, I took it one step further, and called on Lance Miles (our resident 4.0 student). I asked, "Lance, how much is this piece of plastic worth that is holding the water?" He replied, "About 3 cents, Coach."

"Perfect," I said. "Three cents is about right. Now, this is what you need to understand. The video, the press conference, Twitter, and any other social media that you can think of can go viral all at once, but absolutely NONE of this is about us. You see this bottle of water that I am holding? It's a metaphor for what just went down. You guys just told me that water could save your life. If that's the case, then the water in this bottle represents Jesus Christ and His message of love, redemption, forgiveness, salvation, and everlasting life. You see, boys, don't get lost in all the adulation and hype. Never forget the fact that we are just the 3-cent plastic that was, for some reason, chosen to deliver a message. I was chosen for the press conference while you boys were chosen to capture the hearts, minds, and imaginations of not only a city and university, but also a state and other parts of the country. Through the hard-nosed style and blue-collar work ethic, y'all were contagious. Y'all were lovable, and y'all were relatable to people. Even in defeat, you men proved to an entire nation that love conquers all, and yes, all things are possible. My message to you, and what I want to leave you with, is that if it took us losing and then standing up in defeat for a country to hear God's message of love and redemption, then…where do we sign up? I am not only proud, but I am thankful. I love y'all."

Leaving the office heartbroken, I tried to put on a good face as I headed for home. However, body language doesn't whisper – it screams. If you don't know me, I am the worst loser you could ever meet. I have trouble hiding defeat, although I believe those that know me best would tell you that I'm getting better at it with age. After I got home that evening, the Lord spoke to me once more, reaffirming everything that we had just experienced and gone through. This time it was through my precious 13-year-old middle child, Klaire or "Klaire Bear" as she is affectionately known around our house. I honestly believe that the Lord uses children because of their blind faith, and that's exactly what happened. I was pouting, sulking, and moping around the house. Everyone was avoiding me because at this stage in the coaching game, they get it. Finally, Klaire Bear approached me with her joyous smile and asked, "What's wrong, Daddy?" I answered her question with a question. "What's wrong?" I replied. She said, "Yeah, what's wrong, Daddy?" I shot back with, "Well… baby, we just lost a super regional and with that missed our chance at Omaha. That's what's wrong." Klaire, with wisdom beyond her years, immediately said, "Yeah, Daddy, you lost. That's true, but… you guys really won." Now, very intrigued by her response, I said, "Oh yeah? How's that?" Klaire ended the entire conversation right there when she simply said, "Yes, you lost and yes, Florida State is going to Omaha, but no one is talking about Florida State anymore. Daddy, they are still talking about y'all. Y'all won." With that God smiled and winked one more time. I smiled back at Klaire Bear and said, "You're right, baby. You are right about that."

Pictured left to right: Senior catcher Robie Rojas, senior right-handed pitcher Heath Donica, me, and senior second baseman Lance Miles.

Robie Rojas was a "second-chance guy" in the fact that he started his career at Oklahoma State University, left the program after his freshman year, played his sophomore year at Blinn Junior College, and was one of the last players we signed in the 2016 recruiting class. Robie would go on to make the most of his "second chance" by ultimately becoming 1st team All-Conference, winning Southland Conference Tournament MVP in 2017, obtaining his bachelor's degree in criminal justice, and being drafted by the Milwaukee Brewers. Robie is currently a catcher in the Brewers minor league system. Heath Donica was also a "second-chance guy" coming out of Corsicana, Texas. Heath originally gave up baseball and was just a student at Texas A&M University his freshman year in college. Missing baseball, Heath went back home and pitched for his hometown junior college, Navarro, for two years. Heath, along with Robie, was one of the last players we signed in the 2016 recruiting class. Heath went on to become our Friday night starter, won the Southland Conference tournament MVP in 2016, won the Southland Conference "Pitcher of the Year" award in 2017, was named an All-American, and was drafted by the Oakland A's. Heath obtained his bachelor's degree in business and is currently pitching in the Oakland A's organization. Lance Miles really did play with a broken left hand, a broken right wrist, and a torn esophagus at one point. Known as the team's "Alpha Dog" because of his leadership ability and toughness, Lance was a "second-chance guy" as well. He started his collegiate career at Kansas State University and transferred after his sophomore year. Lance was one of the first players I met with upon taking the job at SHSU in the summer of 2014. I offered him a chance to walk on with us and earn a spot. Three years later, Lance graduated as a 4.0 student with a bachelor's degree in business. Lance walked on, paying his own way in the summer of 2014. By his senior season, he received the largest scholarship on the team, not because of his ability, but because he is the greatest leader I have ever had.

Story #2

It's Only Impossible Until Somebody Does It!

All along, through this entire run, our message was, "It's only impossible until somebody does it." We understood, as a team, that to pull off the seemingly impossible we did not have to be better than our opponent 100 times. We only had to be better than them one weekend, and with that we set off to do the impossible. My point that I was getting across is that nobody was in the business of killing 10-foot giants until David came along. A 12-year-old shepherd boy, who was sent to the battle lines to re-supply his brothers with food and water, looked up and witnessed a bully named Goliath taunting the Israelite army in the middle of the battlefield. David responded simply by asking, "Who is it that is defying the living God of Israel?" All the others, intimidated and scared, would not take action, but David said: "Let me go. I will go slay the giant!" With that, David stepped out and met the giant at the battle line. The giant was armed with a 15-pound sword, body armor, a shield so heavy it had to be carried by a shield bearer, and an abundance of cockiness and arrogance. David only had a sling and lots of faith in God. While the giant ran his mouth, David picked up a smooth stone, stuck it in his sling, and whoosh, whoosh, whoosh sunk it into the middle of the giant's forehead. With a resounding "thud" the giant hit the ground and was no more!

Nobody was in the business of beating the Russians in hockey until the 1980 US Olympic hockey team came along. Herb Brooks (a college coach) hand selected a group of seemingly unknown college amateurs, while all the Russians were professionals. Then they set out to do what no one thought was possible. When the country needed it most, a collection of hard-nosed, blue-collar college kids captured the hearts, minds and imaginations of an entire nation. I was nine years old, and my dad let me stay up to watch the finish, and I will never forget it! "Five, four, three, two, one… Do you believe in Miracles? YES!!!" With Al Michaels' famous call, that team proved that it's only impossible until somebody does it.

Why am I so confident that we can and will make the impossible possible? I am confident because I have lived it, and it tells us so in God's word. This program lives by Matthew 19:26, which says, *Jesus looked at them and said, "With man this would be impossible, but with God all things are possible."* For me personally, I grew up in the blue-collar refining town of Texas City, TX, an underdog from the word "go." Nothing was ever given or came easy. Everything worth anything was always earned. I think that's why I have always related to the apostle Paul when he spoke these words to the church of Corinth in 1st Corinthians 1:26-31: "Brothers, think of what you were when you were called. Not many of you were wise by human standards; not many were influential; not many were of noble birth, but God chose the foolish things of the world to shame the wise; God chose the weak things of the world to shame the strong. He chose the lowly things of this world and the despised things – and the things that are not – to nullify the things that are, so that no one may boast before him. It is because of him that you are in Christ Jesus, who has become for us wisdom from God – that is, our righteousness, holiness and redemption. Therefore, as it is written, 'Let him who boasts boast in the Lord.'" Considering this passage, we are a program that plays and competes much bigger than we actually are. We don't have all the amenities you will find at much larger schools, but we make up for that with love, passion, and brotherhood. I learned a long time ago that "passion outdoes logic," and when "gritty meets pretty," well ... pretty is going to get its butt whooped! That's how this passage reads to me and our team. Sam Houston State University baseball is (make no mistake about it) in the business of the impossible!

Take a look at what they have done over the last two years between 2016 and 2017. In 2016, we won the conference title and the conference tournament title in the same year for the first time in program history after starting the season with six wins and 12 losses. We were also the first team in program history to post back-to-back 40+ win seasons. In 2017, we were the first team in program history to begin a season ranked inside the top 25 nationally. We set a new program record and tied a conference record by posting 18 straight conference wins, and became the first team in program and conference history to finish the season ranked inside the top 20 nationally in all five polls. We finished the season ranked as high as 14th in the nation, which was a new program record for highest final ranking. We became the first team in program and Southland Conference history to win an NCAA regional and advance to a super regional. If you can "see" it in your mind's eye, believe it in your heart, wake up every day, punch the time card, and outwork everyone for it, then at that instant, you are in the business of the impossible! Do not ever, ever let anyone tell you that you can't do something. I promise you, ALL THINGS ARE POSSIBLE!

Pictured: The 2017 SHSU Bearkat baseball team celebrating their second consecutive Southland Conference tournament title

There is a quote by Peter Drucker that simply says, "Culture eats strategy for breakfast." Our 2017 team had backed itself into a corner and was in jeopardy of not making the 2017 NCAA postseason. We had been swept twice and lost two out of three twice over the back half of our schedule, so we were in a "win or go home" situation going into the Southland Conference tournament. The boys responded by winning four straight and capturing the Southland Conference tournament title for the second consecutive season. By doing so, we punched our ticket to the NCAA postseason, setting up a historic run in the Lubbock, Texas, regional facing a team we were very familiar with (the Arizona Wildcats) in the first game of the regional. We had squared off with Arizona twice in the Lafayette, Louisiana, regional in 2016 and lost two close games. Arizona would eventually go on to play in the national championship game that year. They were our inspiration going into the 2017 season because we had played them close and knew it was possible after watching the run they made. We won our opening game against them 5-4. The win vs. Arizona set up a winner's bracket game against the host school, Texas Tech Red Raiders. Texas Tech was by far the best team we had played all year. A world series participant the year before, they had a ton of talent and were playing at home. They kicked our butts thoroughly that night, 6-0.

After the game, I let the team "have it" in the dugout by telling them, "If we are just happy to be in a regional, then we can just pack up and go home!" Then I followed that by saying: "I ain't just happy to be here. We came here to win this thing, and this is how it's going to go down. We are going to go back to the hotel and get a good night's rest. Then we are going to wake up, come to the ballpark, beat Arizona, and then beat Tech. We are gonna push this thing to Monday and see what happens." That's exactly what happened! We beat Arizona 9-1 in the first elimination game and then beat host

Texas Tech in the night game by a score of 9-8, setting up a winner-take-all championship game on Monday. We went on to make history that Monday afternoon, winning the championship game 4-3. Like we said all along, we didn't have to be better than any of these guys 100 times. We only had to be better than them one weekend. Talent didn't get us through this; "culture" did.

Story #3

Bearing Good Fruit

John 15:5 says, "If a man remains in me and I in him, he will bear much fruit. Apart from me you can do nothing." We brought a big-time company in earlier this year that specializes in leadership and culture. This company works with MLB teams, NFL teams, and plenty of Power 5 Conference teams. At the conclusion of their evaluation, they came back to us with their findings. They informed us that although we had a few things to work on, we were the #1 culture that they had encountered at any level. Wow! What an honor to hear that about something that so many people have collectively poured so much blood, sweat, and tears into. Their findings blew me away! With all the wins and accolades, what truly stands out is *how* our program is doing those things. We are accomplishing all of this while maintaining a team GPA of 3.3 and leading the way at this great university in community service hours with over 50+ as a team (in 2017). It's one thing to win, but it's another thing to win doing it the right way. I do a lot of public speaking and mentoring, and the number one question I get asked is, "How?" "How do you guys do what you do?" The answer really is very simple. We bear good fruit. How do we bear good fruit? Faith, sacrifice, obedience, and service – the four simple words that this program is built upon, demands, and lives its life by. Faith is being sure of what you hope for and certain of what you cannot see (Hebrews 11:1). Sacrifice – "There is no greater honor than to lay down your life for a brother" (paraphrased from John 15:13). Obedience means more than sacrifice (1 Samuel 15:22). Service – "If anyone wants to be first, he must first become the very last" (Mark 9:35). We dot our "i's" and cross our "t's," check every box, live our life by these four words, and very simply put, we expect to win. I truly believe that because we honor God through our actions, His face is shining down upon us. I started living my life through faith, sacrifice, obedience, and service over five years ago, and I have seen the good fruit of God's loving-kindness, mercy, and grace in everything I have done and everyone He has blessed me to be around.

In 2013, the University of Louisiana (UL Ragin' Cajuns) orchestrated the largest turnaround in the NCAA, going from 23-30 in 2012 to 43-20, advanced to the championship game of the Baton Rouge regional, narrowly losing to host school LSU. The 2013 UL team also boasted the #1 ranked offense in college baseball. In 2014, UL became the first mid-major in the history of college baseball to finish the regular season as the #1 ranked team in the nation in all five polls. The 2014 team finished 58-10, two wins off the all-time record of 60 wins. That team led the nation in total offense as well. The 2014 "Cajuns" had a total of 11 players sign professional contracts. In 2015, I was blessed with my first D-1 head coaching opportunity at Sam Houston State University. In 2016, we became the first team in program history to win both the conference title and conference tournament title in the same season. In 2017, we became the first team in program and conference history to win an NCAA regional and advance to a super regional.

Pictured: Players on the 2018 team loading up after a 12+ hour day gutting houses in a subdivision in Conroe, TX. This neighborhood was totally flooded by Hurricane Harvey in August 2017.

"*Be careful not to practice your righteousness in front of others to be seen by them. If you do, you will have no reward from your Father in heaven. So when you give to the needy, do not announce it with trumpets, as the hypocrites do in the synagogues and on the streets, to be honored by others. Truly I tell you, they have received their reward in full. But when you give to the needy, do not let your left hand know what your right hand is doing, so that your giving may be in secret. Then your Father, who sees what is done in secret, will reward you.*"

~ Matthew 6:1-4

I was adamant that we would help hurricane victims without anyone ever knowing because it's not about us. I instructed our guys not to say a word, and just serve in silence, wherever needed, trying not to bring any recognition to us. I did want to show this photograph for the first time to give you an example of the type of servant leaders we have in our program. For six straight days, below the radar, they used their own trucks, boats, trailers, money, supplies, and equipment to serve those affected by Hurricane Harvey in Conroe, The Woodlands, Liberty, Texas City, Dickinson, Sugar Land, and Cypress. These boys were all over the area, but you will never see it, read about it, or hear about it, except right here. Leadership is service…

Story #4

Transformational vs. Transactional

"My job is to love you. Your job is to love each other." One sentence that I can't tell the team often enough. That one sentence has changed the way I coach and the way I look at coaching. I read those words in a book written by Joe Ehrmann called *InSideOut Coaching*. Tony Robichaux, the head baseball coach at the University of Louisiana, gave me the book one day, told me to read it, and said it would change the way I coach forever. Per usual, Coach "Robe" was right. I spent 430 agonizing days outside of the game I love. The only thing I had ever known, was good at, or ever wanted to do, was stripped from me in an instant. My identity as a man was gone. My entire life, I had formed my identity around Matt Deggs, the baseball player or coach. Now, what I realize is this: Nowhere in the Bible does it call you to live a life in baseball. Truly, the only thing the Bible calls you to do is love the Lord your God with all your heart, mind, body, and soul; and love your neighbor as yourself. That's it. The dangerous part of wrapping your identity into something so fleeting as baseball, business, money, or whatever it may be is when things don't work out or go your way, you are left with a huge void in your heart. Therefore, I promise that if you are not living a Spirit-filled life, you will begin to fill that void with the very temporal things of this world such as alcohol, drugs, gambling, or lust, to name a few. You will also begin to lash out and hurt people out of your own hurt and shame. This is the very reason you see so many successful people stumble and fall. It's not because they lack discipline but because their identity is wrapped up in what they do rather than who they are. I finally realized that baseball is not *who* I am; baseball is only *what* I do. When you come to that realization in whatever you "do," it's very liberating. The first two realizations you need to get to when moving from being a "transactional" coach to a "transformational" coach are these:

1. They are going to win with or without you.
2. You will always need them way more than they need you.

Very humbling, I know. I found this out the hard way. Trust me, these two things are a fact! In 2011 I watched a Texas A&M baseball team that I had (for years) been instrumental in recruiting, building, and coaching, go on to win the Big 12, win the Big 12 tournament, host and win a regional, go on the road to Florida State, and win a super regional to advance to the College World Series in Omaha. Two key words are "I watched." I wasn't there. They somehow figured out a way to do this without me, and there goes that whole "identity" thing again! When you begin to get a grasp on and realize #1, then it makes realizing #2 very logical and easy to understand. If they will go on and win and be successful without you and without missing a beat, then it only makes sense that you will always need them way more than they ever need you. No, you're not "the man." You are ultimately just a small part of the process. The sooner you humble yourself to this fact, the better coach and man you will be. When you come to an understanding of this, the obvious next step is change. For me, the realization was, I can "give a man a fish" by making him do something, or I can "teach him to fish" by getting him to *want* to do something. If you go the first route, you will always get the result you want, but it will be temporary with no value. The second path has staying power with eternal values. Investing in, nurturing, growing, and loving your team is the most important decision you will make.

I have figured out that leading a team, through transformational coaching, requires humbling yourself, living a life of humility, and never, under any circumstances, being afraid to be embarrassed. Let them see your passion! Let them see you laugh, love, cry, sweat, and bleed. Total honesty and humility will lead them to understand who their leader is, what he is all about, and what he stands for. False bravado, putting on airs, and pretenses are all signs of insecurity and are impossible to live up to. We have a saying in our program whenever I screw up or things go wrong because of me or one of our coaches: "Sometimes you just have to overcome the coaching, boys." I say it, the players love to say it, and the other coaches say it too. Everyone laughs, and we move on. The ability to humble yourself, be the real you, and never have a fear of being embarrassed is very freeing. It allows you to truly be the leader that God created you to be. Anything other than the "real" you is a fraud, and kids see through that. It's impossible to live up to, and furthermore, when that view of your self-image is damaged, you will take it out on everyone around you, out of the simple fact that you have been exposed and are embarrassed. True transformational leadership, to me, really boils down to three simple concepts:

(1) Serve them, (2) motivate them, and (3) get them to overachieve by becoming the absolute best together at the stuff no one else cares about. By serving your team, you set an example of putting others' needs before your own, and you prove to them that you will roll up your sleeves and get dirty. You are not untouchable, and at the end of the day you are in this with them. Motivation, they say is like showering… it's recommended daily! The ability to positively inspire, on a daily basis, is key to getting your team to overachieve in everything they do. It's simple. The more people "believe," the more likely they are to achieve! Overachievement is the ability to become the absolute best at stuff no one else cares about. Do so by celebrating every little mundane thing that takes no talent, like showing up early; staying late; working hard; loving your teammates; hustling; and exuding passion, organization, neatness, and service. Little things ultimately add up to the big things.

Developing Men

This game we are privileged to coach and play is so much more than baseball. At the end of the day, our "mission" as a coaching staff is very simple. It's all about developing men. There are five phases that every man must master in becoming a successful professional. We start teaching these five phases to our players immediately in a classroom setting every morning upon their arrival. The first key to any successful endeavor is getting off to a good start.

The Five Phases:

1. **Mind, body, and spirit must be on a full tank.**
    a. Be very aware what goes into your mind.
    b. Be equally aware of what you put into your body.
    c. You must make sure that you are being fed spiritually.
    d. Any pitfall can usually, in my experience, be traced back to one, if not all, of these being neglected and running on empty.

2. **Relationships**
    a. You must work at maintaining healthy relationships.
    b. Only invest in the people that invest in you.
    c. Make time to nurture and grow the relationships that bring value to your life.
    d. Distance yourself from high-maintenance, one-sided relationships.
    e. Nothing will end a career faster than a toxic relationship!

3. **Appearance**
    a. You must work on *how* you present yourself, doing so with a spirit of excellence.
    b. Physical appearance
    c. Dorm/Apartment
    d. Vehicle
    e. Locker
    f. Clubhouse
    g. Dugout
    h. Sloppy only breeds more sloppy!

4. **Responsibilities**
    a. Have a willingness to show up, punch time card, and work.
    b. School
    c. Service
    d. Baseball
    e. Hard work pays, and it is the secret to becoming a successful man.

5. **Finances**
    a. Become a good steward over what you have worked for and been blessed with.
    b. Good credit
    c. Living debt free
    d. Investing/Planning
    e. Finances ruin more relationships than anything else.

These five phases all feed off each other. Excelling at one allows you to excel at another, but failing at one will create a domino effect that will ultimately cause you to carry metaphorical "baggage" everywhere you go. Our goal as a team is to be baggage free at everything we do. In order to accomplish this, we teach the mastery of what we call, The Three M's:

1. *Manage* your time and be organized.
2. *Master* our routine.
3. *Make* a positive impact.

No successful man lacks any of these, and it always leads to the successful mastery of the five phases of becoming a successful professional.

Pictured: Me and senior catcher, Robie Rojas, prior to the first game of the 2017 super regional at Florida State University.

We have one simple message to the players every day. "Play hard, have fun, and love your teammates." We can control all of these. Very few things in baseball and life are truly in our control. Our mission is to be the absolute best at the things we control, and not really worry about the things that we don't. We don't have a rule book or a policy manual. Instead, we have a "standard." It hangs outside the clubhouse, and it's up to every player and coach to get above the bar, and live in the *"standard ..."*

The Standard

All things are possible
We bring energy
I like to help, I like to serve
No excuses
Never out of the fight
Expect
Ready to work, ready to lead

"My commitment will only run as deep as my belief in our standard."

Chapter 2
The Beginning of the Journey

"For I know the plans I have for you," declares The Lord,
"plans to prosper you and not to harm you, plans to give you
hope and a future."
~ Jeremiah 29:11

Story #5

Texas City

I was born and raised in Texas City, Texas. What you need to know about Texas City is that it's just as much a "mindset" as it is a place. Texas City is a blue-collar, working-class town of about 40,000 situated on the gulf coast of southeast Texas, just across from Galveston Island.

The people of Texas City are honest, hard-working, tough, and loyal. Their work ethic defines them. It's an "us" versus the world mentality with a huge chip on the shoulder of just about everyone. Most folks there come from "the school of hard knocks."

My parents grew up in Texas City, my wife's parents grew up there, both sets of grandparents lived there, and most of our extended family lived close by. Texas City is best known for three things:

1. Petro-chemical plants line seven miles of the Texas City coastline. Texas City is the 5th largest port in the country. Almost everyone you know works at one of these refineries or chemical plants. If they don't, they are probably doing something associated with them.

2. The Texas City "disaster" happened in 1947 when a ship carrying tons of fertilizer caught fire and blew up in the port, causing a chain reaction that ultimately killed more than 500 people. To this day, it's one of the largest man-made disasters in the history of the United States.

3. The Texas City Dike is the world's longest man-made pier. The Dike is an asphalt road bordered by granite rocks on each side. It juts close to seven miles into Galveston Bay. On the Dike, you will find bait camps, shrimp boats, fishermen, and folks just looking to hang out on the water. Growing up, I spent many days fishing on the Dike with my dad, grandpa, and friends. Those are some of the best memories of my childhood.

My family was no different than anyone else from Texas City. In fact, I was the first one in the entire family to graduate from college. Both of my parents worked blue-collar jobs. My mom worked at Sherwin Williams paint store, the Parks & Recreation Department, the local Baptist church, and later owned a flower and gift shop. My dad drove an ice truck, managed a chain of convenient stores, sold Canon copiers, and then worked for 30+ years at a local chemical plant. We lived paycheck to paycheck, but my sister Gina and I never "wanted" for anything. My parents worked extremely hard to provide for us, and for everything we didn't have they made up for with love and time spent. My mom was my biggest supporter, and to this day still is. No matter how tough things got, she always had a way of looking on the bright side and making you feel as if things were going to be okay. I was born with severe asthma and every allergy you can think of. There were many trips to the doctor's office, late-night emergency room visits, and even hospital stays. Through all of it, my mom made me feel as if I were bulletproof. She always would say, "I promise you are going to be OK." Every time, I believed her, and every time she was right. My mom worked incredibly hard, and was very loyal and faithful to our family. She was known as the "pushover." I could talk my mom into almost anything. If I ever needed something or wanted to do anything that was remotely questionable, I would ask my mom. I remember talking her into letting me drive my dad's standard transmission truck (by myself) to the store and back when I was only 14. The only time you knew you were in trouble with my mom was when she would utter the very scary words, "Just wait until your dad gets home!"

My dad was my hero from the very beginning. Larger than life both figuratively and literally. He has always commanded respect when he walked into a room. Dad was a super athlete that played all three sports but excelled in football. Starring for the Texas City Stingarees as an all-district nose guard, he had several opportunities to play in college on scholarship. However, those dreams were quickly dashed when his adopted father walked out on him, his mom, and sister during his senior year in high school. Left with only one option, my dad stayed behind, got a job on the Texas City Dike, and supported his family. To this day, I truly believe my dad is such a great father and grandfather because of his own tough experiences growing up. Dad was adopted by the Deggs family the night he was born. He never knew his biological parents. In fact, I remember when I was around 12 years old, some friends of ours tracked down his birth mom, dad, and siblings. His birth father had died in his mid-40's in a boating accident. His birth mother and sister were living in the same county as we were. A family friend called his birth mother to ask if she would like to meet him, but she adamantly declined. Years later he would learn that both his biological mother and sister had passed by reading about them in the local newspaper. He never had the chance to meet them, and this has always broken my heart for my dad. Determined to be the father he never truly had, my dad was incredible! Always there, always wise, always loving, and always did absolutely whatever it took to take care of our family. My dad was my first and greatest coach, and to this day I get a text the day of every game with "his" lineup. No one knows this, but he has written out many a lineup from Texarkana to Sam Houston.

Besides my dad, my grandfather, Verbon "Rock" Giddings, was the man I most looked up to or aspired to be like. Rock, as he was known because of his "rock-like" build, dark black hair, and steely blue eyes, was in every sense of the word a "man's man." My Grandpa (as I called him), was a boxer in the US Navy, served in WWII, and then hung drywall on Galveston Island until a few years before he passed away at the age of 85. I can remember as a 10- or 11-year-old kid going to work with my grandpa. He would hang drywall, and was known as the absolute best on the Island. I would do the menial jobs like haul supplies, sweep, or pick up trash. I absolutely loved going to work with him, not just because I idolized him, but because he would let me chew tobacco, say the occasional cuss word, and always found time to "wet a hook" with me (go fishing) in a canal behind one of the houses we were working in. I thought this was the coolest thing ever! Grandpa only had one rule: "Just don't tell your mom."

My wife Kathy and I were high school sweethearts. We started dating in the summer of 1988 and have been together ever since (29 years in all.) However, our relationship almost didn't get off the ground. Although I had a crush on her for a while, Kathy didn't share the same sentiments, and I was afraid to ask her out. My mom, God bless her, finally coaxed me into working up the courage. Finally, I got her number and called. After beating around the bush on the phone, Kathy beat me to the punch and abruptly asked, "Are you trying to ask me out on a date or something?" Taken aback, I responded, "Well, if you want to go out, I guess we could go do something." A few days later – June 9, 1988, to be exact – I picked Kathy up, met her parents (Ernie and Jane), and we headed to Almeda Mall. We went out to eat and watched the movie *Big* starring Tom Hanks. From that moment, the summer after our sophomore year in high school, we were inseparable. We went to different colleges and our early career paths took us in different directions, but we always found a way to make it work. After dating for nine years, Kathy and I were married on June 28, 1997. Although our journey together has not been easy, to say the least, Kathy remains the love of my life and my best friend. She has blessed me with three incredible children: Kyler 18, Klaire 14, and Khloe 12. Kathy has stood by me, no matter how difficult. She is a saint, with many jewels in her crown! The amazing part of our relationship is that my parents and Kathy's parents were high school sweethearts at Texas City High School. They all grew up together. My dad graduated with Kathy's mom, and both sets of our grandparents all knew each other. Texas City – it's who we are, and it's the tie that binds us.

Pictured: Circa 1984, Texas City Dike, L to R – me, 12 or 13 years old; my dad, Jimbo, and one of my best friends growing up, Beau Mayne.

Some of the best times of my life were spent fishing on the Dike with my dad, grandpa, and friends. My upbringing in Texas City helped to shape me into the man and coach I am today. "You can take the boy out of Texas City, but you can never take Texas City out of the boy."

Story #6

The Competitor

From the time I could walk, all I ever wanted to do was play sports and compete. My first trip to the hospital, for stitches, came when I was just four years old. Watching Sunday football with my dad in the living room, I was pretending to be the running back, took off, and dove directly into the corner of our wooden coffee table. Strangely, I still remember that. Although it was my first trip to get stitched up, it would definitely not be my last.

I was never a particularly gifted athlete. I played every sport and was always known for my passion, hustle, grit, intensity, and willingness to do absolutely whatever it took to win. I was ill-tempered and a horrible loser from the get-go! There were always fist fights, arguments, and just about any type of dust-up you can think of from the time I was five playing in the neighborhood or sandlots. This attitude would continue throughout my career. This edge, intensity, attitude, chip on my shoulder, or whatever you want to call it, is a double-edged sword. It can get you into a lot of trouble, or it can also serve you to overachieve.

When I was eight years old, I can remember a baseball game getting rained out in my first year of "pee wee" league. When my dad called the house around 4pm to inform me the 8pm game was rained out, I was already in full uniform. I hung up the phone, turned to my mom's brand-new sofa, and with cleats already on, kicked a huge hole in the left side of it. I then went into the garage, got my dad's rake and hoe, jumped on my bike, and pedaled the 10 minutes to the Pee Wee East ballpark. I began working by myself on the field. After about an hour, I jumped back on my bike and pedaled home. My dad was home from work by then, and I informed him that I had fixed the field "good enough" and thought we could play. He said, "No, son. They already canceled the game, and how did this hole get into your mom's new couch?" After that, out came the belt!

When I was 14, after an all-star game which we lost, I took my hat off while the coach was speaking to the group and ripped it in half. Everyone turned around and just stared at me in disbelief. Upon seeing this, my dad, who was one of the assistant coaches, made me apologize to the team, buy a new hat with my own money, and sit out the next game. In 1986, my favorite team, the Houston Astros, was in a pivotal game five in the National League championship series against the New York Mets. I was 15 years old at the time and playing freshman football. After practice, I could not get home fast enough to see the completion of the game. The Astros ultimately gave up a lead and lost in 16 innings. When the right fielder, Kevin Bass, struck out to end the series, I fell out of my chair onto the ground and started crying. My dad, sitting on the couch next to me, very simply said, "Get up." I shot back with, "No!" He said, "I am only going to say it one more time. Get up, and stop acting like a baby." Boldly, I came back with: "No! I'm not getting up! That's b_ _ ll sh_t that we lost that game!" "That's it!" he said. "Go to your room. You are grounded for a week!" With that, I may have been the first kid ever to be grounded because the Astros lost! The next day on the front page of *The Houston Post* was a huge picture of a dejected Astros team in the dugout after the loss. I cut the picture out, and it hung in my room for years after that. I made myself a promise that it would hang in my room until I made it on the team and helped get them over the hump!

When Kathy and I were around 18 or 19, we were playing Monopoly in my parents' home. I had been in the lead the entire game and was acting very arrogant about it. Every time I would land on one of her properties, I wouldn't give her the exact amount. I would give her five to ten dollars more and tell her to "keep the change." Inevitably, after making a series of bad investments, I found myself strapped for cash and now on the losing end. The tables were turned! Kathy, who is probably as competitive or more than I am, was now letting me have it. Things were getting more heated with every roll of the dice. After landing on one of her properties with a hotel, I was now out of money and needed a loan. She said, "Nope!" I then flipped the board over and hollered, "Get out!" Yes, embarrassingly enough, I kicked my future wife out of my parent's house over a game of Monopoly. Probably another first…

For all the trouble and heartache that my over-the-top passion and competitiveness got me into, there were lots of times that it also served me very well – from championships to over-performing, playing with injuries, and even leadership. My sheer passion, competitiveness and consumption with winning was always the fuel for my fire.

We won the pee wee championship when I was eight, won the minor league championship when I was 10, won the major league city championship when I was 12, won the pony league championship when I was 14, and we also won the regional all-star championship that same year. I made the American Legion team after my freshman year. I made the high school varsity team and started as a sophomore, and in my senior year we brought home the first district title in baseball in over a decade, narrowly losing out to Andy Pettitte and Deer Park High School in the playoffs. My freshman year of football we went undefeated and won the district championship as well. I was never really a standout on any of these teams as much as I was a leader. I was the guy that pushed, demanded, would call you out, and drove the train. I was not one of these guys you see today that says they "lead by example." No, I stirred the pot both physically and verbally. Not being the most talented, you have to find ways to catch the coach's eye and "get in the frame" so to speak. My work ethic and passion were second to none. No one could match my passion, so no one could outwork me. I was the kid that was up at 6am calling friends and knocking on doors while most were still in bed. My friends thought I was crazy, and I'm sure their parents weren't too happy with getting woken up early on a Saturday! I would fight you, literally, in order to win. Many scraps took place at the ballpark and on the football field. Teammates or opponents, didn't matter to me. I would barrel roll into second base to stay out of a double play, run over the catcher, get into a collision, hit you after the whistle, foul out, or whatever it took to win and stay in the picture.

My leadership always came naturally, and it wasn't the popular kind. I had no problem making waves, challenging people, saying what needed to be said, or doing what needed to be done. I had a one-track mind, and all I wanted to do was win! I would call and run my own practices in the offseason, many times at the dismay of my teammates. We played high school ball at Robinson Stadium, a city park that was kept under lock and key. Many days, we would beat the lock off the gate with a bat so we could practice. On one occasion, after showing up and finding it locked again, we were so irate that we drove my buddy's car through the gate, and we practiced. I couldn't stand it when guys were late, didn't go hard, went out the night before, made excuses, or missed time because they said they were hurt. I always took pride in going as hard as I could, 1000 miles per hour, no matter the sport. My sophomore year, my right leg was in a cast because I had broken my ankle. After about two weeks in the cast, I went in the garage, got my dad's hacksaw, and cut the cast off so I could go to American Legion tryouts. My dad was furious, not because I went to tryouts, but because I cut the cast off that he had paid for. I got my nose shattered in a football game against Galveston Ball High, went back in the game, only to be removed after turning the wrong way on a running play. It turned out I had a concussion too. Every finger and thumb has been broken on my right hand at various times, only to tape it up and keep going. I have no ulnar collateral ligament (UCL) in my right arm. That was blown up many years ago, and I never had it fixed.

One of the dumber things I've done to compete was in 2008. Jeremy Talbot and I, while coaching together at Texas A&M, loved to play golf in the offseason. "JT" beat me up on the course pretty regularly, and on this particular day my game was absolutely terrible. After hooking yet another drive in the rough, I decided to punch the golf cart. When I looked down at my right hand, my knuckle was shoved back near my wrist, and my pinkie finger was pointing the wrong way. I looked at JT and said, "Dude, check out my hand." He took one look and quickly exclaimed, "You're a freaking idiot, Deggs!" I pulled my pinkie back in place and attempted to play three more holes. At the turn (9th hole), I informed JT that I was done and was going to see our team doctor. The team doctor, after confirming to me as well that yes, I'm an idiot, told me he wanted to put a pin in it and cast it. I told him: "No way. This is the offseason and the only time of year that JT and I get to play golf!" One week later, JT and I were back at it. I wrapped my hand with athletic tape, and he let me tee up every shot!

College, for as hard as I had worked, was uneventful for me as far as baseball was concerned. After having delusions of grandeur of how it would go, my bubble was burst when I went relatively unrecruited and walked on at Alvin Community College. That first year, I lived at home and drove the 30 miles or so every day to Alvin. I played sparingly as a freshman, but always continued to push and work hard. My sophomore year at ACC was more of the same. The only difference was that our coach had awarded me with a scholarship, and I lived with teammates in an apartment just off campus. Although I worked, practiced hard, and performed well when given the opportunity, I was still nothing more than a part-time player as a sophomore. Even though my time and experience at ACC were not very positive, I am truly thankful looking back, because it gave me perspective on two very important things: (1) I didn't get to play all the time even though I deserved to, so I have always been able to relate to guys that don't get in the game as much as they believe they should, and (2) I learned how not to treat players. Our coach was a terribly poor communicator and always had double standards for guys. This infuriated me. To this day, I use the negative experiences I had at ACC to help me understand where players are coming from.

Undeterred by my experience at ACC, I was determined to "press on" in pursuing my dream of not only playing in college but playing in the big leagues. The only problem was, after my sophomore year, I was back at square one. No one was calling, and I had very few opportunities at that point. At that time, my dad contacted Northwood University, a small

(NAIA) school in Cedar Hill, Texas, that had recruited me some out of high school. One June morning after working from 6pm to 6am, my dad loaded me up on no sleep and drove me the five hours to Northwood University to work out for them. I performed well, they offered me a scholarship, and I said yes!

Northwood, at the time, was somewhat of a baseball factory. The NAIA ranks were known at that time as somewhat of an outlaw league, chock-full of guys that had talent. However, it was mostly unfulfilled and lots of guys were working on their last chance. We had something like nine guys go out and play professionally during my time there. I loved every second of my two years at Northwood. Guys were flawed, but we loved each other, were super talented, played extremely hard, and we were led by Coach Pat Malcheski. Coach "Mal," as he is known, is to this day one of the greatest examples of a strong Christian man that I have ever been blessed to know. I love Coach Mal, and he is still a huge influence in my life today.

The highlight of my college years came my senior year in 1994. I was a team captain, hit .308, and led our team in assists while playing third base every day. This would be considered a very average year for most, but for me it was the highlight of a very unassuming college baseball career.

Little did I understand that I had already been blessed more than I realized. This blessing had happened the year before in 1993, my junior year at Northwood. Our pitching coach was Rob Childress, a former pitcher at Northwood who was only two years older than I was. Rob and I had a strong player/coach respect for each other and had quickly become close friends. I didn't realize at the time that the best was yet to come!

Pictured: 1983 Triangle Pharmacy Oilers, Texas City Major League "City" Champions. Coaches pictured L to R Jimbo Deggs, JC Matus, Jim Mayne. I am top row, far right along with 3 of my best friends to this day: Donnie Higgs, middle row far right; Sean Matus; middle row next to Donnie; & Beau Mayne, bottom row second from the left.

The "Oilers" started off that season 0-3 (true underdogs) but never flinched, came all the way back, and captured the prestigious "City" Championship. I was given the honor of eulogizing Coach JC Matus (Sean's dad) several years back at his funeral, and I had all the former "Oilers" stand up and be recognized. When times became the toughest for me personally, Higgs, Matus, and Beau were there every step of the way and still are!

Story #7

Finding a Way

It was May 1994. Out of eligibility and only had a couple of weeks left until I graduated. I had absolutely no clue what I was going to do with the next chapter of my life. Then I got a call from Rob Childress. Rob was now the head coach at Texarkana Junior College, and he was looking for a hitting coach. He thought I would be a great fit and that coaching was definitely in my future. Rob, who is very persuasive, invited me to drive the three hours from Dallas over to Texarkana to visit, take a look around, and sell me on the prospects of becoming his hitting coach. I drove over, we spent the day together, and Rob offered me my first job. I think it was going to pay around $5,000. At the end of the visit, I informed Rob that I would love to be his coach, but there were just two things I needed to do first: (1) I was set to graduate and get my degree in two weeks, and (2) I was not ready to give up my dream of playing professional baseball – I wanted to attend a tryout camp that was coming up the following week. After informing Rob of my plans, he responded quickly with, "Great. I will see you in two weeks, after you graduate." He totally dismissed my idea of playing professionally, probably because he had watched me play for an entire year.

The Texas-Louisiana Professional Baseball League was in its first year of existence, and they were set to hold four massive "open call" tryout camps across the country in the Northeast, Florida, Texas, and California. At the conclusion of the camps, they would hold a draft to fill the rosters of the eight initial teams, which were in Mobile, Alabama; Alexandria, Louisiana; Beaumont, Texas; Tyler, Texas; Amarillo, Texas; San Antonio, Texas; Edinburg, Texas, and

Corpus Christi, Texas. The tryout in Texas just so happened to be held in the Dallas-Fort Worth area, right where I was living at the time. My teammates and I had been reading about this tryout in the paper for weeks. We were all excited for the chance and anxious for the opportunity to continue our careers. The tryout was a three-day event with cuts to take place each day, culminating in a draft of the guys that were left on the third and final day. Dallas Baptist University was the host of the tryout I was set to attend. "DBU" is literally a 10-minute drive from Northwood. On the day of the tryout it rained continuously, the field was muddy, and prospective players littered the field like ants. More than 500 players showed up, each with the hope of fulfilling his dream of becoming a professional baseball player. After we all checked in, received our ID numbers, loosened up, and were ready to go, we were informed that the field was too muddy and we were changing sites to Dallas Jesuit High School. Now in a mad scramble, everyone got directions (no GPS or cell phones then), loaded up, and set off to find the high school. It was intense because they were going to start the camp with or without you. I showed up just in time to run the 60-yard dash. All professional camps were set up and run in the same manner in order to measure your ability in running, throwing, fielding, and hitting. The reason they were run in this way and in this order is because they were going to make cuts at the end of each "measurable." We all knew this fact, so nerves were through the roof. Everyone was anxious to prove what they could do. When over 500 guys stand in the way of what you have worked your entire life for, it's "dog eat dog" at that point. I was never known for my foot speed; my best time in the "60" was a 7.0. The big league average is 6.8, so I knew that I had to find a way to make it through the 60. On a muddy field, somehow, I mustered up a 6.9. I couldn't believe it! Yes, I made it through the first cut!

Next was the defensive evaluation. In this portion, everyone goes to their position and the scouts measure how well you field and throw. I played third base, so I went to third, and there must have been a line of 25-30 prospective third basemen. My number was low, so I was situated in the back of the line. The first thing we were set to do was take throws from all the outfielders who were throwing from right field to third base. After a couple of outfielders threw to third, I was getting antsy. In my mind, I was telling myself that I would have to make a way to get noticed. The very next throw to third, my opportunity came and I jumped at the chance. Still waiting my turn in the back of the line, an outfielder uncorked a wild throw that was heading up the line 15-20 feet from third base. Instinctively, I pushed the guy in front of me down, jumped in front of the guy whose turn it was, and put myself in position to knock down the throw and keep it in front. The ball short-hopped me and hit me right square in the throat! I never flinched. The camp came to a stop as the scouts and managers had seen what just happened. One manager, Charlie Kerfield, came over to check on me. He said, "You OK, dude?" Barely able to speak, I answered, "Yeah, man, I'm fine." Charlie said, "You're one tough SOB!" I said, "Nah, I just love to play." With that, I made the second cut. First, the 60, and now this. It's almost like it was meant to be, but I still had two more days, three cuts, and a draft to make it through.

The next day, along with the rest of the guys that were left, we came back and played two games. They made a cut after each game. In each of my three at-bats that day, I hit a hard line drive for a base hit and made every play. I was on fire, and all I kept telling myself was, "Just don't blow this!" After that, instead of searching out opportunity, I basically just faded into the background, hoping that what I had already done was enough. The third and final day came, and now we were down to around 100 guys. We played a game, and sticking to my plan, I only got one at-bat, in which I walked and made a couple of plays in the field. Then they made the final cut. Those of us that made the cut were told to go to lunch, come back at 1:00, and they would let us know who was drafted into the league. With emotions running high, we gathered into the football bleachers at Jesuit High School and waited to find out which of our baseball careers were going to continue. A three-day camp that started with more than 500 guys was now down to around 75. Finally, the eight managers came out and, one at a time, they began to inform the remainder of us who had been drafted for their teams in each of the four rounds. In the fourth and final round of the draft, my name was called by the Mobile Baysharks! In that moment, the course of my life was changed forever. I made two phone calls. The first call was to my dad. The second call was to Rob to inform him that he wouldn't be seeing me in two weeks. We still laugh about this story.

I was blessed to get to play three years professionally, and although we were an "independent" minor league team, which meant we had no affiliation with any major league team, the baseball was equivalent to AA minor league ball. My second year in Mobile, we had a working agreement with the Boston Red Sox. During these three years, I really came into my own and truly started to become the player that I always knew I could be. I guess I was just somewhat of a late bloomer. In fact, my final year of playing in 1996, I hit .348 for the Tennessee Tomahawks of the Big South League. Although I never came close to getting to *the big leagues*, these three years of pro ball would have a profound effect on my coaching career, both positive and negative. On the positive side, I had the opportunity to play for and play with a ton of guys that had played in *the big leagues.* This experience proved to be invaluable from the standpoint of soaking up knowledge and learning the game at a very high level. In fact, my second year in Mobile, our manager was Butch Hobson. Butch had played in *the majors*, managed the Boston Red Sox, and was a legend in the state of Alabama, having played both football and baseball for the Crimson Tide. On the football team, he played for legendary coach Paul "Bear" Bryant. Butch was a "players coach" with more baseball knowledge than any man I had ever met. Butch and I quickly developed more than a player/manager relationship. We became great friends. I respected and admired Butch for the way he managed and his passion for the game. I believe he respected my hard-nosed approach, work ethic, and passion. Butch was one of my early mentors in the game, and I am still thankful to this day for having had the opportunity to learn from him. Our relationship has spanned well over 20 years. In fact, we signed his son, KC, to a baseball scholarship in 2008 while I was at Texas A&M.

The three years I spent in professional baseball were some of the most fun times of my life. To me, there is nothing better than getting to play a game you love and get paid for it at the same time. I also met some of the greatest friends I have ever had, while playing. Many of these relationships I still have to this day. Although we may not talk all the time, these guys are like brothers, spread from coast to coast. There is no fraternity quite like baseball.

While my time in Mobile and Tennessee proved to be beneficial in the furthering of my baseball career, it also led me down a path that I almost wouldn't make it back from. For all the positives of professional baseball, there are also pitfalls and traps that are very easy to fall into. As dedicated as I was to the game, I quickly started to fall prey to the destructive habits that can come with such a carefree lifestyle. Games would begin at 7:00, be over by 10:00, and then it was on! Beer and food were always readily available in the clubhouse or on the bus. We would sit around, break the game down, and just shoot the bull for an hour or two. Then it was off to get dressed and head out. We would hit bar after bar through the wee hours of the morning. We would sleep until noon, get up, go eat, and make it to the ballpark in time for early workout at 2pm. This would soon become my routine for the next three summers. As much "fun" as it was at the time, it would ultimately prove to be highly unproductive, especially for someone with my tendencies who only knows two speeds – "fast and faster!"

Pro ball was truly a double-edged sword for me. On the one side, it was the opportunity of a lifetime, fulfilling a dream, learning so much about the game, and making so many incredible friendships. On the opposite side, there was ego, as well as arrogance and living in perpetual sin through alcohol, lust, and self-gratification. Sooner or later something has to give. You can't run an engine at full throttle all the time.

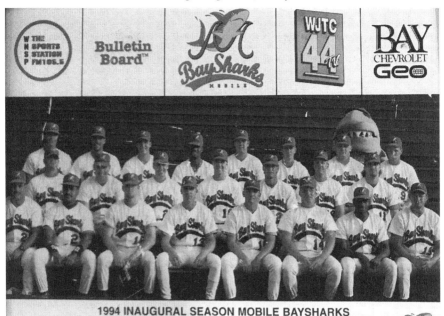

1994 INAUGURAL SEASON MOBILE BAYSHARKS

Pictured: Team picture of the first team in Mobile Bayshark history. I'm located bottom row, 5th from the left. Mobile, Alabama, is an incredible town, and supported the Baysharks like we were a big league team. My time spent in Mobile holds some of the best memories I have in baseball.

Story #8

My Identity

Pro ball affords one the opportunity to live a free-spirited life, all the while being wrapped in somewhat of a bubble, guarded from the outside world four or five months of the year. Although I knew in the back of my mind I wasn't nearly good enough to play in the big leagues, I kept chasing that dream with absolutely no regard for life after baseball and what I would do next. All that changed one morning after a long night out drinking with my teammates. I was woken by a phone call from my good buddy, Rob (Childress). By this time, he was the pitching coach at Northwestern State University in Natchitoches, Louisiana. Rob asked me one question: "Are you still interested in coaching?" Still hung over and sleep deprived from the night before, I answered, "I don't know, Rob. I'm still playing." He once again hit me with, "You and I both know that's not going to last." Then he ended with: "If you will go take the GRE and make an 800 on the test, we can pay for your master's degree while you begin your coaching career. I sent you something in the mail. Look at it, and get back with me." There was no e-mail back then, so I waited a couple of days and sure enough, a handwritten letter arrived from Rob. This letter changed the course of my life.

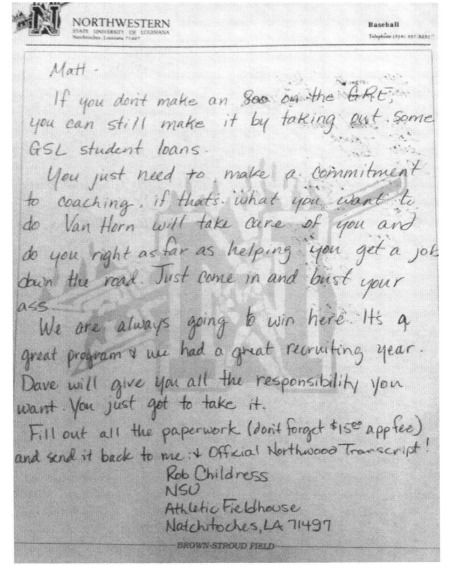

NORTHWESTERN
STATE UNIVERSITY OF LOUISIANA
Natchitoches, Louisiana 71497

Baseball
Telephone (318) 357-5251

Matt -

If you don't make an 800 on the GRE, you can still make it by taking out some GSL student loans.

You just need to make a commitment to coaching. If that's what you want to do Van Horn will take care of you and do you right as far as helping you get a job down the road. Just come in and bust your ass.

We are always going to win here. It's a great program & we had a great recruiting year. Dave will give you all the responsibility you want. You just got to take it.

Fill out all the paperwork (don't forget $15⁰⁰ app fee) and send it back to me + Official Northwood Transcript!

Rob Childress
NSU
Athletic Fieldhouse
Natchitoches, LA 71497

BROWN-STROUD FIELD

After reading this letter, I made a deal with myself. I would go to the nearest Sylvan Learning Center and take the test on the next off day that we had. If I passed the test with an 800 or better, then I would give up playing and start a career in coaching. I called Rob, told him thanks for the opportunity, and informed him of my reasoning. Later the next week, I found the closest Sylvan Learning Center in Mobile and signed up to take the GRE on one of their computers. At the time I hardly knew how to turn on a computer. Therefore, I was excited to figure out that the test would be scored immediately, so I would know where my future was headed that same day. The test took me more than four hours. It was grueling and felt like taking the SAT all over again. The room was packed with people taking the test, and they passed out scratch paper for the math portion. I remember watching everyone else use the scratch paper. I didn't know enough math to use the scratch paper... so I jotted things down, then erased them to look busy like I knew what I was doing. Then I just winged it! Finally finished, I closed my eyes and hit the submit button. Guess what score popped up on the screen? The exact score I had to make was staring back at me – an 800! I took this as a sign and called Rob to inform him, "I will be there for the start of school."

Rob's letter was 100% accurate. He and Coach Van Horn did take care of me and gave me a ton of responsibility. We did win, and I did begin my master's courses getting most of them paid for. The greatest business decision I have ever made in my life by far was taking Rob's advice in that letter.

In December of 1996, I did something that I never thought possible. I walked across the stage and received my master's degree, living proof that all things truly are possible. In June of 1997, at the end of that same school year, Kathy and I got married. We rented a house just off campus. Rob and the rest of our family spent an entire weekend helping us move in and set up our first home. About six weeks prior to that, I had interviewed for the head coaching job at Texarkana Junior College – the same "JC" where both Rob and Coach Van Horn had previously served as head coach. Coach Van Horn had made a phone call to the president of the school, Dr. "Cheesie" Nelson, and gotten me an interview. As it turned out, I didn't get the job. Dr. Nelson hired Todd Shelton. However, six weeks after taking the job, Todd decided to take the head coaching job at Eastern Oklahoma Junior College. We had been in our new home together for two weeks and finally had the last mini-blind hung when I received a phone call. It was Dr. Nelson, and he said, "You still want to be the head coach at Texarkana College?" Without asking a single question, I responded, "Yes, sir, I sure do!" That weekend Rob and I started the entire process over again. We packed up the entire house, rented a U-Haul truck, and moved everything Kathy and I had to Texarkana.

At the age of 26, I was now a head coach. Just two years after taking Rob up on his offer, I was now running my own program. Texarkana proved to be an incredible training ground for a young head coach, as I was tasked with doing just about everything. Looking back, I am very thankful for my time at Texarkana College – it was a great place to "cut my teeth." We didn't have much. My first salary was $28,500. Kathy and I thought we were rich. The team didn't have our own field. We had to use a city park, and we were in charge of all the maintenance. There was only one place for the players to live, and it was called the "coupe" because it was an old Kentucky Fried Chicken warehouse with bunk beds installed. We only had nine scholarships in comparison to most of our competition who had at least 15. I only had $5,000 to pay an assistant, but I love a challenge and knew, based on the past success that both Rob and Coach Van Horn had experienced there, that we could win and win big. As it turned out, Kathy and I had a great five-year experience in Texarkana. Our oldest child, Kyler, was born there at CHRISTUS St. Michael Hospital in 1999. We won the conference championship in

2001 and advanced to the school's first-ever Junior College World Series in Grand Junction, Colorado. Again in 2002, we won the conference championship and narrowly missed a repeat trip to the world series. We made strides off the field as well. We went from nine scholarships to 15. I also convinced the school to purchase a small apartment complex right across the street from campus for the players' residence. Then we secured over $100,000 to make our off-campus city ballpark as nice as possible. Thirty-five of our players went on to play at four-year schools highlighted by Hunter Pence. Yes, that Hunter Pence!

For all the success we were having, my personal life was still heading in the wrong direction. Kathy and I didn't have a happy marriage, we didn't belong to a church, and I spent all of my time living hard and continuing to glorify all the wrong things. I was incredibly harsh, demanding, and very much a transactional leader and coach at the time. My sole purpose and identity were wrapped up in baseball and my own personal glory. Looking back, I had to be incredibly tough to live with, work for, and play for! The worst part is, I was having success (or so I thought). At the end of the 2002 season, I got a call one evening from Coach Van Horn, who was now the head coach at the University of Nebraska. Coach Van Horn informed me that he was taking the head coaching position at the University of Arkansas and was offering me the opportunity to become his hitting coach and recruiting coordinator. At the age of 31, seven years after taking Rob's advice, making a personal deal with myself and starting a coaching career, I was a hitting coach and recruiting coordinator in the SEC.

To say our life was changing and changing fast would be an understatement. I was going from the fast lane to the even faster lane. The SEC is 24/7, 365, and "dog eat dog." It's survival of the fittest. For a guy with an all-or-nothing personality with his personal identity wrapped up in his career, however glamorous it may appear, it's a recipe for disaster. Mix in alcohol, late nights, arrogance, ego and selfishness, and you have a recipe for total destruction. That's the path I was on and spiraling down quickly.

My first year at Arkansas, I was over my head and out of my mind living fast, hard, and loose while coaching the exact same way. Nothing had changed, and although we won 35 games, held our own in the SEC and made a regional, I know beyond a shadow of a doubt that I was even more impossible to live with, coach with, and play for. How and why Kathy and Coach Van Horn kept me around, I will never know! They both had plenty of reason to cut and run.

In January of 2004, it all changed. I was tired of living a life fueled by my own selfish arrogance and self-gratification. I rededicated my life to Christ, thanks in large part to a former University of Arkansas football player, Josh Foliart. Josh is the most dynamic man I have met in my life. He reminds me of a modern-day Apostle Paul. When you look at him, you can literally see Christ in him. Josh worked at Arkansas, ministering to coaches and athletes. For over a year, I had run from him. I resented Josh because he lived in the light, and in my heart, I knew I was living in darkness. I gave my life to Christ at the age of 10 in the Baptist church. I knew Christ, but ever since I was a teen I had lived in darkness and as an enemy of the cross, only satisfying my own selfish desires. I guess I was finally at the end of my own rope and sick of Josh's persistent pursuit. After I returned from Christmas break, I finally, reluctantly agreed to meet with him for lunch. Then right there at the AQ Chicken House, over fried chicken and iced tea, I rededicated my life to Jesus. From that point on Josh and I were inseparable. He became my mentor, and over the next year Josh fed and taught me the Word of God. Prior to our friendship, I had hardly opened a Bible. Now I was living daily in the Word. I owe my life to Josh. As you will learn, his time spent with me would ultimately help in literally saving my life.

The 2004 season was one of the greatest seasons I have ever been a part of as a player or coach. First, I quit drinking, dipping, and cussing overnight, cold turkey. Second, I lived for Christ in everything I did. Third and most redeeming, I was a part of a team that had several players and two coaches come to know Christ as their Lord and Savior that season – wow! That 2004 team was the absolute, most amazing team I have ever played for or coached. Picked pre-season to finish 10th out of 12 SEC teams, all we did was win the SEC championship, host a regional, host a super regional, and advance to the College World Series in Omaha, Nebraska. That season was highlighted by the most miraculous comeback I have ever been a part of: Facing elimination in our own regional, Wichita State had a three-run lead in the top of the 9th inning with two outs and no one on base. Then suddenly, we had the bases loaded with two outs, setting the stage for our catcher, Brady Toops, who was the most faithful, loyal, God-loving kid on the team. On the first pitch Brady sent a low and away change-up to left field. The left fielder immediately started sprinting back toward the wall, and just as he was reaching up to catch it, boom! He ran out of room, hit the wall, and the ball barely cleared the fence for a game-winning grand slam home run. It was the most miraculous thing I have ever witnessed on a baseball field. I get goose bumps just writing about it.

We would go on to win the regional, beat Florida State the next weekend in a super regional, and in two short years we had helped the University of Arkansas get back to the College

World Series. The highlight of the trip for me was celebrating our daughter Klaire's first birthday in Omaha. What a thrill! I will never forget that.

Once again back on top, but this time I was doing it the right way.

Pictured: The 2002 Texarkana College Bulldogs after the final game of the Region XIV Tournament. That was the last game I ever coached at "TC"; we lost a heartbreaker, narrowly missing a return trip to the Junior College World Series for a second straight year. That team was chock-full of grinders and some very talented players. Ten players went on to play D-1 Baseball & nine more went on to play professionally. Highlighted by Hunter Pence, third row, second from the left, who is still in an 11-year big-league career and a two-time World Series champion.

Chapter 3
From the Top to the Bottom

"There are two kinds of people in this world, those that are humble and those that are about to be."
~ Rich Donnelly (longtime Major League Baseball coach)

Story #9
Aggieland

The 2005 season was an absolute kick in the gut, to say the least. Although I was living strong, making good decisions, and following the Lord, this season would be an incredible test of will and faith. We returned most of the team that had won the SEC championship and taken the University of Arkansas to the College World Series. The 2005 season at Arkansas started off incredibly. We were an offensive juggernaut. We had it all including speed, strength, and power. We were on fire from the start! After going to #1 ranked South Carolina and taking two out of three, we jumped to #5 in the national polls. It was a forgone conclusion around most of the league that we had "the team" and were heavily favored to repeat as SEC champions for a second straight year. Those expectations came to a halt following a series against Mississippi State when we had to suspend two of our best hitters for the remainder of the year. I won't go into specifics, but the point is, we were forced to play the remaining three quarters of our schedule without our two best players. At the time of the suspension, these two guys were literally leading the SEC in almost every offensive category. Those who think that a team can pick up, carry on, and just keep winning without their two best players are fooling themselves. We did our absolute best to keep it rolling, but to say we limped to the finish would be an understatement. At the same time, due to the pressures of having to get into a regional in the rigors of the SEC, I could sense myself becoming more and more transactional. I was starting to slip back into my old ways with the occasional drink, foul language, and lots of "what have you done for me lately" coaching. Once again, looking back, my identity was starting to migrate towards baseball.

We somehow got into a regional, in large part due to Coach Van Horn, who is still the best "back against the wall" coach I have ever seen! Never make the mistake of counting Dave Van Horn out of anything. He is a natural-born winner – at anything! We went to The University of Texas regional for the second time in three years, and somehow we pushed the Longhorns all the way to the "if necessary" championship game, narrowly losing. The Longhorns would go on to win the National Championship that year.

While we were competing for a championship at the end of the 2005 season, there was a lot going on behind the scenes. The Texas A&M job had come open towards the end of May, and quietly tensions were mounting as to who was going to get that job. A&M is located two hours from where Kathy and I grew up in Texas City. Kathy graduated from A&M in 1994, and my sister Gina also graduated from there. For Kathy and me this would be like going *home*, a place we hadn't been in years. I had made my interest in the job very clear to Coach Van Horn, although we both agreed that I didn't stand much of a chance. He knew my affinity for going back home. As it turned out, Rob (Childress), who was at the University of Nebraska at the time, was also highly interested in the job. After an exhaustive search, towards the end of June 2005,

Texas A&M named Rob Childress as head baseball coach. Rob called, not even hours after that, and said, "Let's go!" I didn't hesitate!

Something I wasn't expecting happened the very next day as the news of our impending move was circulating through our family. It's wild to think about now. I got a call from Gina, my sister and the most faithful person I know. She and her husband Tyson are missionaries who are both very faithful to the Lord. Gina called me upon hearing the news that we were leaving to go to A&M, and naturally I thought it was a congratulatory call. Quickly she went on to say in no uncertain terms, "Do not take that job." I said, in my arrogance, "Are you serious? This is the chance of a lifetime!" Gina simply responded, "I just have a feeling this isn't the right time for you and your family to move. Stay where you are." Upon hearing that, I said, "Whatever!" and hung up. What ego and arrogance. My sister's words would later prove very prophetic, as I believe the Lord was using her to speak directly to me one final time before I exercised the "free will" He has given us here on earth.

On June 28, 2005, Rob and I both landed at the same time at the airport in College Station. Leaving our families behind temporarily in order to set up shop in "Aggieland," we began the process of turning around a very proud program. The day we landed was Kathy's and my wedding anniversary. She was also eight months pregnant with our third child, Khloe. I left my wife on our anniversary, eight months pregnant, with two other young children, and a house to sell. Coaches' wives are unsung heroes who never get enough credit for all they do caring for their families and often holding it all together on their own.

In the meantime, Rob and I jumped in head first. We worked 15-hour days recruiting, getting organized, looking at personnel, and at the same time looking at houses. It was my responsibility to look for and buy the home we were going to live in. It doesn't sound like a big deal, but it's an arduous, time-consuming task with lots of pressure. Rob and I lived in the Hilton hotel for the next six weeks. I went back to Arkansas briefly just in time for the birth of our beautiful baby girl, Khloe, on July 25. I went back 10 days later to load up the family and make our move to College Station.

The 2005-2006 season, my first at A&M, would eventually wind up being one of the hardest seasons I have ever experienced. Looking back, I am very thankful for having gone through it. It turned out to be an invaluable learning opportunity. Although I was not drinking at the time and somewhat following the Lord, I showed up once again very arrogant and operating in a transactional mindset. I was the "big shot" and A&M was, in my mind, blessed to have me there. Instead of coming in and humbly accepting the situation for what it was, a rebuilding process, I was truly arrogant enough to believe that I could personally change my side of the ball (offense) overnight. Boy, was I ever mistaken! Here I was, coming off lots of success at Arkansas, and I was foolish enough to believe that I could help turn A&M into the same thing overnight just because I was there. How immature and egotistical, to say the least. Instead, when things didn't go my way, when the players didn't buy in, or the fans didn't like something I did, I turned on them, protecting my fragile image at all costs. In hindsight, I honestly believe I gave the players I inherited and was responsible for a negative experience because of my transactional ways. I also didn't mesh with the fans from the get-go. Much of that had to do with my intensely aggressive offense. It was different from anything they had ever seen under legendary head coach Mark Johnson. In the process, I lost the players and many of the fans. If I could go back, I would accept the situation for what it was, be more patient, and do my best to see the situation from their perspective. Unfortunately, I did the opposite of that. The team finished the 2006 season 25-30 and missed the conference tournament, and hit around .240 as team that year. Everyone, it seemed, wanted to run me out of "Aggieland" after only a year. Looking back, I don't blame them. It was a very inauspicious beginning to say the least.

Two things came out of that season, however, that would change the course of my coaching career. I have never been the smartest, but I have always had a gift for figuring out how to get things done from a practical standpoint. First, we had an incredible recruiting class. Although we lost Clayton Kershaw and Zach Britton to the draft, we still brought in 20 top-notch players the following year that would orchestrate the largest turnaround in the NCAA. This, combined with Rob's leadership & vision, would lay the foundation for 11 straight regional appearances, six conference championships and two trips to the College World Series for A&M Baseball since 2006.

The players had a lot to do with that incredible run of success, but the guy behind it all, Rob Childress, truly doesn't get enough credit. Rob is one of the most consistent, organized, and caring men I know. He is an incredible leader and builder of men. He is gifted at building lasting relationships, and if my son played baseball, Rob Childress is definitely a man I would want for his coach.

Secondly, after not getting it done offensively and knowing that I had always had success, I was determined to map out a system that was organized, defined, and would provide a game plan for success. I spent the entire summer of 2006 thinking, plotting, and mapping out this system. Thus, *The Pack Mentality* was born. *The Pack* has been wildly successful over the years and something that I have passed down and taught coast to coast from the high school level to Fortune 500 corporations. *The Pack* has been implemented nationwide not only in multiple levels of baseball, but in the business world as well. *The Pack* was truly a game changer for me, and little did I know it would prove invaluable in the weeks, months, and years ahead.

What would follow the 2006 season was nothing less than validation and pure redemption. The 2007 and 2008 teams were nothing short of incredible. On the other hand, I was now drinking again off and on, our family didn't have a church community, and I was at the height of my transactional ways. I was only living for myself. Was "worldly" validation and redemption really something I needed to hang my hat on at that time, or was it only serving to feed the big, bad wolf inside of me?

Pictured: Me and Texas A&M head baseball coach, Rob Childress, in the dugout during a game at Olsen Field. Rob and I began at Texas A&M together June 28, 2005.

Rob Childress and I were best friends when we went to Texas A&M. To this day, Rob is still one of my best friends. He provided me and my family the opportunity of a lifetime. I firmly believe that all anyone needs is an opportunity, and after that it's up to them to decide what they make of it. I will always be grateful to Rob for that chance. He is one of the best men I know.

Story #10

Redemption

Coming off a miserable first year, 2007 was a year to remember. Just a few months prior, we finished the season 25-30 and could not generate any offensive momentum. Now, fueled by the outcome of the 2006 season along with plenty of naysayers, the chip on my shoulder was bigger than ever. I was a man on a mission to prove everyone wrong, and I would stop at nothing to do it. I coached with a vengeance and nastiness about me that was palpable. We had 20 new players on campus, and I was teaching all the hitters *The Pack* way. I was determined to get my point across at all costs. We worked and worked and worked, and then we worked some more. I pushed the limits, coached hard, was very demanding, and tried to pull every ounce of ability out of them. They were tough, athletic, strong, and faster than most. We functioned as a team, and everyone loved and played for each other. However, if that concept didn't play out the way I thought it should, I would crush them, reinforcing how things were now going to be. Although I loved that team in 2007, I would have to ask aloud, "Was I a guy back then that I would trust my own son with?" The honest answer years later is simply, "I don't know." Yeah, we won. We set records offensively, guys went on to play professionally, we won championships, and I loved those guys – but what values was I teaching them under my charge? Had I truly been smart, mature, and grounded enough, I would've taken the time to stand back and watch. I would have watched how Rob worked, moved, coached, and cared for those boys. Unfortunately, I didn't. I was arrogant enough to think I knew it all, and I was going to do it my way. My way would prove to work, but what I have realized is that it was temporary. There were no lasting, redeeming, or eternal values to what I was doing. What was I doing? I was self-motivated, self-serving, transactional, and living with an image of myself that was a lie. Although we were experiencing success, it was not going to be a lasting way of doing things for me personally. The front I was beginning to perpetuate was one of a tough exterior that put "team," winning, and success above everything, all the while behind the scenes, I was beginning to put my own family and team second to my own personal agenda.

The 2007 season was one of proving everyone wrong. That team quickly became one of the most dynamic in the country. In fact, they set the all-time Big 12 stolen base record by swiping 151 bases. They led the conference in several offensive categories, won the Big 12 tournament, and were selected as a regional host in the postseason. What a difference a year can make! We went from 25-30 and completely missing the postseason to being ranked as one of the top teams in the country.

At the Texas A&M regional, we hosted LeMoyne University, Ohio State, and the #2 seed, the University of

Louisiana. I can still remember us feeling like we had been slighted in our regional because they sent "UL" to us. The Ragin' Cajuns had a phenomenal team headlined by current big leaguer Jonathan Lucroy. We won the first game vs. LeMoyne but dropped a heartbreaker to UL in the second game, losing on an incredible play by their left fielder. He leaped and robbed Craig Stinson of a game-winning home run in the last inning. Heartbroken, we came back the next day and beat Ohio State in game one, setting up a rematch with UL in the nightcap. We beat UL 4-1 to set up a Monday winner-take-all championship game. We scored first and never looked back. The Aggies won the regional 5-2 behind a dominating performance by pitcher Kyle Thebeau, who threw a complete game striking out 13. Of course, I had to watch the final six innings from behind the bullpen wall since I had been kicked out in the third inning for arguing a play at the plate. I was such a hothead back then.

Something else significant happened the night of the championship game that I wouldn't find out about for several years. We were in the visitor dugout and UL was in our dugout because that's the way it was done back then. Therefore, like it or not, UL had access to our clubhouse. The UL head coach, Tony Robichaux, would share with me years later that he went in and studied *The Pack Mentality* that was hanging up on the wall. Admittedly, this concept was intriguing and stuck with him in the back of his mind. Although I didn't know Coach "Robe" at the time, he now had a newfound respect for what I was doing. Four years later, I would realize that Coach "Robe" being in our clubhouse that night and reading about *The Pack Mentality* was no accident.

A few days following the regional, we loaded the bus to make the one-hour trip to Rice University in preparation for the super regional. I remember like it was yesterday, looking over at Rob and saying, "We are going to Omaha – can you believe it?" We lost two heartbreakers at Rice. Our expectation of a trip to Omaha was put on hold, but we proved that A&M Baseball was back, and once again a force to be dealt with in college baseball.

The next year was even better. Though we lost several players to the major league draft, we returned a great nucleus and filled the gap with more dynamic players along the way. The culture and expectations were becoming ingrained, and we were well on our way to big things. The 2008 team had a little bit of everything – including speed, strength, power, defense – and we could really pitch. That team worked, battled, played, and competed extremely hard at everything. Like the previous year, they quickly became one of the more dynamic offenses in the country, and as a team they pulled off something together that had never been done before. They managed to set a Big 12 record, winning 16 consecutive conference games in a row. Unlike the 2007 team, the guys in 2008 managed to win the Big 12 Conference regular season title. Although we stumbled at the conference tournament, we were well on our way to hosting our second straight regional. We hosted University of Illinois-Chicago, Dallas Baptist University, and (#2 seed) the University of Houston. We beat UIC in the first game 15-1, then took down UH 22-4. We only needed one more win against UH the next day to win our second straight regional. We came out on that Sunday evening and lost a heartbreaker 4-3. Once again, we were set to play a winner-take-all Monday regional championship game. We won 13-5 and advanced to the super regional in Houston vs. the Rice Owls. We were confident and playing at a very high level. There was never any doubt. We were going to get it done this year and advance to the College World

Series. Like the year before, Rice had other plans. They took us down in two straight thrillers. We lost 9-7 and 6-5, blowing leads in both games for the second year in a row. Rice was going to Omaha, not us.

Although both seasons ended in heartbreak, there was no doubt that in three short years we had put A&M Baseball back on the map and certainly back into national relevance. For me personally, I was 36 years old and at the top of the mountain, or so I thought. We were coming off back-to-back Big 12 championships, our offense was one of the best in the country, and our recruiting was going great. After one of our wins in the regional, I met with representatives from Mississippi State and interviewed for their head coaching position. I didn't think it could get any better. This was coming easy. I was the man (so I thought). I was well on my way, and nothing, in my mind, could stop me. I treated people like I had no time for them. I was arrogant, cocky, and full of myself. I was trying to live up to an image that was not only false, it was unattainable. Consequently, the pressure was mounting behind the scenes, and adversity was just around the corner.

Pictured: The 2007 A&M baseball team dogpile following a 5-2 win over, ironically enough, the UL Ragin' Cajuns. From finishing last in 2006, to hosting and winning a Regional in 2007, it truly felt like sweet redemption! Not seen in this photo is me. I was jogging onto the field from behind the visitors' bullpen. I had been kicked out of the game six innings earlier for arguing a call at the plate. Even though I knew assistant coaches were not allowed to argue calls, I couldn't help myself because it was all about me. If I had been wise at the time, I would have taken notice of something... the team is going to win with or without me. Later that night, I would celebrate this huge accomplishment by glorifying alcohol, instead of the Lord. What an immature, selfish, fool I was.

Story #11

Adversity Hits

The funny thing about adversity is that it doesn't make you a man. It only reveals where you are as a man, for the entire world to see. Then it gives you a chance to do something about it. Adversity, unbeknownst to me, was about to serve up a wonderful opportunity, if only I would have responded the right way.

Having gone from the bottom of the Big 12 to the top in one short year and then validating that ascent the following year, the pressure was starting to mount. As the old saying goes, "The hard part isn't getting to the top; the hard part is staying there." The inability to get past Rice and advance to the College World Series was weighing heavily on me. Both years we had put together dynamic offenses, but when it mattered most, we had a problem getting it done. We couldn't overcome Rice's daunting pitching staff, and I was taking it personally. Had we been able to put the ball in play more and come up with a couple of big two-out hits, I just knew we would have won. Couple that with the fact that I had run us out of an inning or two coaching third base, and I was feeling the heat, self-induced heat. I felt terrible for the players and coaches because they deserved better. I had been overly aggressive, and I should have had our hitters more prepared to face what they were going to face in Rice. Once again, arrogance and overconfidence led me to believe that I could go in and have a hand in helping us get to Omaha. That line of thinking cost us big!

Meanwhile, two huge events were beginning to unfold in my life. The first was personal and financial, the second was about my best friend and the man I looked up to the most. This set the stage for what would prove to be a very trying and difficult year.

Towards the end of the summer of 2008, my mom drove up from Texas City to spend the day with our family. We took the kids out to a lake and then went for a "Sunday drive," winding up in Conroe. We decided to stop and grab a bite to eat before driving back to College Station. We had a wonderful time together, and the entire day seemed innocent enough, until about two weeks later. Kathy opened the mail to find a returned check from the bank. The check was written to Wal-Mart for $3,000.00. The handwriting was not ours and we obviously knew that neither one of us had ever written a check in that amount to Wal-Mart. Immediately we knew there was a problem. We contacted the bank, and they informed us they understood and would not pay the check. We hoped that this issue was over, but the following week we received another check and another and another... We contacted the authorities in hopes to get to the bottom of it. They could not provide many answers except to tell us that someone had stolen our identity. Ironically, my identity had already been stolen. For a guy that was searching for his own personal identity, to have it literally stolen now makes me chuckle at the thought of it. What ensued the following three months was nothing less than time consuming and absolute frustration. No one could get to the bottom of it, no one. To make matters worse, because Kathy was still living in Arkansas at the time that we moved, everything was in my name. Even though Kathy was a stay-at-home mom at the time, she was unable to work on it because everything was in my name. Every bank account, every credit card, everything with my name on it was affected, all the way down to my driver's license. Every time I thought we had gotten to the bottom of it, another charge would pop up somewhere. I spent almost every day, for two or three hours, for close to three months, trying to get our identity back.

During that time, I got a phone call from my mom. She was calling to inform me that my grandpa, who was my best friend and one of the men I most looked up to, was in the hospital in west Houston and that it didn't look good. My Grandpa was 85, strong as a bull, and hardly had a gray hair in his head. I honestly thought he would easily live to be 100, but there he was, lying in the hospital bed battling congestive heart failure. He looked like a shell of himself. I had never seen this man look weak, and now he was lying in the intensive care unit, weak, frail, and struggling to breathe. It shocked me when I saw him. Immediately I lost it and began to sob right there in front of him. For the next three weeks, I pulled triple duty going to practice, driving to the hospital, and working on getting my identity restored.

The last time I saw my grandpa, he was doing better. They said he was recovering and they were sending him to a rehab center to get back on his feet again. I will never forget the last words that my grandpa spoke to me. As I was leaving, I looked at him and said, "I will see you later, Grandpa." He said, "OK, Bubba. I'll be seeing you, Bubba. I will be looking for you." That was the last time we ever spoke. We never told each other that we loved each other. I guess it was just understood.

On October 25, 2008, Kathy and I were at a Halloween party when my phone rang. It was my dad. All he said was, "He's gone." I said, "Who's gone?" He answered, "Your grandpa; he died tonight." Kathy and I left the party, got in the truck, and I lost it. I punched the steering wheel so hard that it bent in half. I couldn't believe it. I was devastated. A week later I gave the eulogy at his funeral. He would now be 94, and I still can't believe my best friend is gone.

Right after that, the Conroe police called and said they busted a ring of identity thieves and they were sure that these were the guys who perpetrated the crime against me. They explained how they did it. When my mom came to visit that day earlier in the summer, the restaurant where we ate scanned my debit card. Then they sold the scan, and the thieves got into my account and created their own checks. Working with someone on the inside, they would go buy thousands of dollars of merchandise with the fake checks, only to then go pawn it. What an emotional time! Just when you think you're bulletproof, life proves that nobody is.

On December 31, 2008, Kathy & I hosted a New Year's Eve party at our home. Everyone brought their kids, we cooked, heated the pool, swam, and sat in the hot tub. We had a fire going, and the drinks were flowing heavily. The baffling part is, I had not been drinking a whole lot recently. This night would be different. We had one of the wildest New Year's Eve parties the neighborhood had ever seen. We sat in the hot tub drinking till after 3:00 in the morning. At some point, we cut a tree down in the backyard to keep the fire going, and that's about all I remember. Several of our friends had the spent the night, and no one got up before 1:00pm, except for me and one of my lifelong friends who was up from Texas City. He was a fellow believer, and he looked at me and said, "Dude, we are crazy. We can't be acting like this anymore." I agreed totally. I felt horrible, mentally and physically, as he and I picked up the mess for the next two hours. We both agreed that this was it, and we were going to put the bottle down.

At that time in my life, I drank in spurts. I was determined that this was it. We had a huge season right around the corner, and I was going to dedicate it up to baseball and my family. So, in January of 2009, I quit drinking... again. That promise to "dedicate it up" would last a whole 10 days. After I spoke at the Texas High School Coaches Convention about *The Pack* offense, I immediately left for one last hunting and fishing trip in southeast Texas before the season was to begin. While I was there, I wound up drinking all three days. I was so disappointed in myself, and I recommitted once again that I was going to put the bottle down. This time I lasted about two months.

In the middle of all this, another first happened. We became the first team in Aggie baseball history to begin a season ranked as the preseason #1 team in the nation. In January of 2009, *Baseball America* tabbed Texas A&M the #1 team, the favorite to win it all! Fueled by this #1 ranking, I was more determined than ever to grow up and get my life on track.

That commitment would be short-lived. We had an up-and-down season from the get-go. We couldn't find our footing, and never really lived up to the expectations that year. For the first time in two years, we weren't hitting, guys weren't buying in, and the leadership that had been so steady over the previous two seasons now seemed to be lacking. I fought and battled the urge for as long as I could, but when your identity is wrapped up in what you do and not in who you are as a child of God, you really stand no chance. So, in late March I gave in and picked up the beer bottle once more to drown the despair I was living in from a season of disappointment. If your mind, body, and spirit are not on a full tank and your identity is tied to the temporary things of this world, trust me, these decisions are inevitable. With the renewed drinking and lack of discipline, I was effectively throwing in the towel, and why? Because we were having a rough season? Big deal! I wish I were more of a man back then and less of an immature, self-absorbed jerk. My coaching had reached the height of transactional; I was an emotional roller coaster that ebbed and flowed based on results, very inconsistent, and no one knew what they were getting from one day to the next. The only consistent thing about me was the numbing that would take place at night courtesy of Miller Lite.

We limped our way to the finish line by getting swept at Oklahoma to finish the regular season. We didn't fare much better in the Big 12 tournament and punctuated the season by finishing third in the Fort Worth regional, hosted by Texas Christian University. A long year that began with a stolen identity and the death of my grandpa had mercifully come to an end, or so I thought.

A month later, after ending a very disappointing season, we had to say goodbye to Jeremy Talbot. "JT" was our recruiting coordinator and coached our hitters with me. For personal family reasons, he had to leave baseball and head back to his home town. JT and his family were from south Louisiana. Within days, they packed up and headed home. I was devastated for JT and his family. I couldn't believe what was happening. Gone was my right-hand man and one of my best friends and neighbors. I understood why it happened, but it sent my world spinning and put an exclamation point on a year full of adversity.

Pictured: Klaire, Kyler, Kathy, Khloe and me. The seemingly happy family had it all – a big job, a big house, and a life of comfort. They also had a man in the center of it who was beginning to live a lie. My wife and kids saw it coming, but there was literally nothing they could do to stop it. I was feeding the big bad wolf inside of me and he would stop at nothing to "get his." It hurts to look at this picture even now as I type, knowing the pain that I caused. They deserved so much better.

Story #12

Lost at Sea

Reflecting on it seven years later, I can see there were several "triggers" that would lend themselves to pushing me over the edge, ultimately resulting in my total destruction. Had I been more mature at the time, I could have handled things differently. I should have known that I was predisposed to alcohol addiction. Knowing my grandpa battled it too in his younger years, he was the man I was determined to be, warts and all. I should have understood the life I was living did not mix well with my temperament and inclinations. I should have had our family in a church, but I didn't have time for that. The perfect recipe had come together for my getting lost.

The interesting part of getting lost at sea is that it happens slowly, over time. You slowly drift away from your mark on the shore until you look up and can't see land anymore. Guess what? You're lost! By the time you realize it, it's too late. That's exactly the way it happened to me.

I went from giving up drinking in January of 2009... again... to not being able to put it down over the next several months. Why? Several factors lead to my demise, but I couldn't connect the dots at the time. I was too self-absorbed, lacked mental stability, and was running on an empty tank spiritually. I literally couldn't see that I was lost, I mean gone, until it was too late.

Putting two and two together, it took several events over several years to finally bring me down. Beginning with the most recent, the 2009 season where the ball was dropped, I was determined to get us back where we were as a team. I proceeded to put the 2010 group of hitters through the most arduous, grueling, fall practice season that you could imagine, often pushing things to the very edge. Coach Paul "Bear" Bryant and the Junction Boys would have been proud of what I put these guys through. It was an absolute grinder. Consumed with my own personal failure, I was determined never to go through a season like that again. The fall of 2009 weighed heavily on me. I knew I was pushing the limits. I was doing it without JT, who was going through his own personal challenge back home in Louisiana. I couldn't get over how we, as an offense, had underachieved. Therefore, I pushed the hitters beyond their limits during the day, and would isolate at home in the evenings by dousing 10-12 beers. Over time, this became my new routine. I would go as hard as I could at work, get to the beer store as fast as I could, drink 2 beers before I even got home, and then isolate from my family while they ate dinner without me. I drank, then I would eat around 9 or 10pm, pass out, and do it all again the next day. Watching this go on day after day in the fall of 2009 and early 2010, Kathy begged and pleaded with me to get a grip on my life. My answer was always the same: "I don't have a problem. I'm just stressed and need to unwind, babe. Quit nagging!"

I remember it like it was yesterday. As I would drive to the beer store after work, I had to pass the exit for my house to get there. A quiet voice, who I believe was the Holy Spirit, would speak into my heart right before the exit to my house. I heard, "Just go home. Go home. You can do it." Every time, instead of taking the exit, I continued straight to the beer store. If only I had listened to the voice in my heart.

After several months of this, Kathy drew a line in the sand. She sat me down and informed me that through my actions, I had divorced myself from my family and that I could either choose my family or choose alcohol. She went on to say there would be no more drinking, and if that's what I chose to do, then I would lose her and the kids. The decision, as hard as it is for me to admit, was easy. I chose to drink, and with that I chose a life of sin, lies and self-absorption that often comes with addiction. What I couldn't see at the time was that Kathy was speaking for everyone – my parents, her parents, our family, and close friends including Rob. It's a strange feeling for everyone but you to know you're a complete mess.

The "perfect storm" had come together. My life was spinning out of control. I was "lost at sea." To complicate matters, I have lived with Obsessive Compulsive Disorder (OCD) since I was a kid. I didn't realize it until I had to seek help for it as a young adult. At the same time my life was unraveling with alcohol, I was also on two different prescriptions for OCD, neither of which should be mixed with alcohol, but I didn't care. In my mind, I would do whatever it took to numb myself to avoid the reality of the situation. That's what happens when you are transactional, selfish, and only motivated by your own personal glory. I had no spiritual foundation and had lost my moral compass somewhere along the way. It truly was a dark, dark place.

The moment Kathy drew the line in the sand, I knew we had a huge problem. Up to that point I did most, if not all, of my drinking at home. I never drank at work or enjoyed going out and drinking. I loved drinking alone and isolating. My personality is such that if you order me not to do something, odds are I'm going to do it. I have always been that way. When Kathy put her foot down, I knew that to feed my cravings, I would have to become more creative and cunning. With that came even more lies and deceitfulness. I was officially a liar now, and the shocking part was how easy it became. Instead of coming home, I would say *I'm working late*. Instead of going somewhere with the family, I would say that I needed to stay home and work. You get the idea. They were all lies to fill my selfish desires and continue to live a life of self-gratification and destruction.

Before you know it, you are so tangled in a web of deceit that you can't keep up with it all. It's absolutely exhausting and miserable. I now tell people when I speak, "The only thing more miserable than living in an actual prison with four walls where someone sent you, is living in a prison of your own making with four invisible walls where you sent yourself."

Now fully submersed in addiction, cravings, lies, and deceit, I was truly living a double life. I was a coach by day and a liar/con artist by day (and night). By this point, I wasn't the only one in on the act. By the middle of the 2010 season, the closest people in my life were in on it too and desperately trying to reach me. "No problem here," I would say to them. The more people came down on me, the further out to sea I would drift. My logic at the time was that I didn't have a problem. They were the ones with the problem. If they would just leave me alone, then I would be fine, and one day this will all pass. I was famous for lying, mostly to myself, and believing it. I would pray every night for God to save me, and then I would crack open another beer. I would tell Kathy that sooner or later God will take this from me and we will all be fine. God never did stop me or save me, at least not on my terms.

To compound the life I was living was the fact that we were winning and hitting (again) in 2010. I took that, in my disturbed way of thinking at the time, as validation. "I don't have a problem. Look at us. We just won the Big 12 tournament again." We won 43 games, hit .300 as a team, slugged .460, stole 106 bases, and had three future first round major league draft picks on the team. We took the University of Miami, on the road, to the championship game in the regional.

In my mind, I was the man. We were back, and I had it going on. I was arrogant enough to believe that I was the reason for all of this. I really thought that I was responsible for all the success, and this team would not be able to do any of this without me. Wow! That is tough to admit, even harder to write about, but all of it is true. Once again, egotistical, arrogant, and fueled by selfish pride – all the while living a lie off the field. In hindsight, I was severely underachieving on the field too.

The last game I ever coached with my best friend, Rob, we walked through the gates at the University of Miami's baseball stadium in a knock-down, drag-out verbal fight. Rob didn't pick the fight; I did. I didn't agree with a player he was determined to play that day, and I let him know my feelings right then and there in front of anyone within earshot. I was out of my mind! Eaten up with selfishness and entangled in too many lies to even keep up with, I would lash out at anyone. I still feel regret to this day that that was the last time I coached a game with my buddy. He should have fired me right then and told me to go sit on the bus. He had every right to do so.

To show how self-absorbed I was at the time, several hours earlier from my hotel room in Miami, I phoned Rob to inform him that I had just heard that the UH job was open and I wanted to go after it. I did that, just hours before the biggest game of our season. I had the nerve to put this on Rob's plate and make it all about me. I really didn't consider how it looked, nor did I honestly care. I was that selfish. After we got beat by Miami that day, our season was officially over. Now, in the Miami International Airport, awaiting our flight home, I isolated myself. Yep, I isolated myself from the rest of the team after our most disappointing loss of the season. For me, I was on to the next best thing, becoming the head coach at the University of Houston. While the team waited together for the plane, I stood in the corner and worked the phone. It was plainly obvious to everyone what I was doing. What a jerk I was – an entitled, arrogant, addicted, narcissistic jerk.

The next few weeks were spent recruiting, fueling my addiction to alcohol any way I could, and chasing after the UH head coaching job, as if I were in any condition to become a head coach. Kathy and I are from the Houston area and UH, at that time, was a dream job for me. Somehow, I got my foot in the door. In early June, I drove down and met with representatives from the University of Houston.

They made a great decision in their hiring process by not hiring me. I can say that seven years later, but at the time I was devastated when they called to inform me they were going with someone else. I had convinced myself that I was the best man for the job and was sure that I would be the coach they would hire. Knowing the way I was living back then, I really cannot believe that I thought I was the right man for the job. I really can't!

After that, what resulted was a total free fall. Instead of picking myself up by the bootstraps, thanking God for the opportunity, learning from the experience and carrying on like a man, I did the opposite. I became even more bitter, started acting like a bigger jerk, and all the while drowned my sorrows in even more alcohol. This unraveling was now taking place in front of everyone in my life, and it was becoming painfully obvious that I needed help… to everyone, that is, but me.

I talked with Rob and Kathy, who were both quickly coming to the end of their rope. They both agreed that I needed to get away for a while, clear my head, sort things out, and just take a break. I planned a trip to Atlanta. One of our former players had just been called up to the big leagues by the Braves. I was set to spend a week out there, watch him play, relax, and get my mind right. I flew to Atlanta for the week, but I don't remember much else. Instead of this being a trip to reconnect with a former player, celebrate his accomplishments, and do a personal inventory of my own life, I used the trip to drink and stay drunk for an entire week. I totally neglected my family while I was gone and didn't accomplish anything besides digging myself into an even deeper hole that was becoming impossible to get out of.

After returning home hung over, bitter, and mad at myself, I was willing to meet with my family. I agreed that something had to be done or I was going to lose my family, friends, team, and job. In July of 2010, I did something that I thought I would never do, something that only other people do. I checked into rehab.

Pictured: Me and a 10-year-old Kyler in the dugout before a game. Kyler is now 18 and a senior in high school. This picture is priceless as Kyler is a hero to me. Although he is sitting on my lap, he was the man of the house at the time, more than should ever be asked of a 10-year-old boy. When your daddy is a drunk, someone has to help take care of the family. Kyler stepped up and did that. I will always admire and look up to him for that. He was a man when his daddy wasn't.

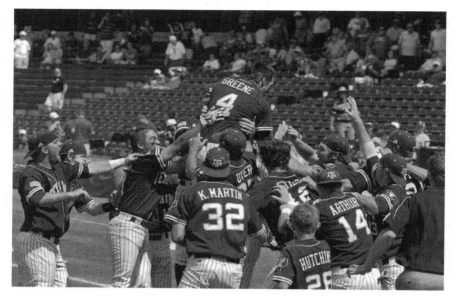

Pictured: the 2010 Aggies celebrating Brodie Greene's 10th-inning, game-winning "walk-off" home run to win the Big 12 Conference tournament – the last time I would celebrate a championship with the Aggies. Ironically, I sat in the corner of the clubhouse and just soaked it all in. I was the last one to leave after everyone got dressed and got on the bus. I still don't know why, but I could feel something telling me this was it. What a great team. They deserved so much more from me.

Pictured: Me with Brandon Hicks in July of 2010. Brandon played for us at A&M in 2007 and was making his big league debut with the Atlanta Braves. In an effort to get away and get my mind right, I flew out and spent a week watching Brandon and the Braves. While they played, I sat in the stands and drank, then drank some more and then some more. What should have been a wholesome celebration of a lifetime achievement was ruined by my own selfish behavior. I flew out there looking to turn things around and came back home even worse.

Chapter 4
The Desert

Pride goes before destruction, and an arrogant spirit before a fall.
~ Proverbs 18:11

Story #13
I'm Done!

I will never forget that awful July morning. There I was, standing in my kitchen having to look my three young children in the face and tell them Daddy was going away to rehab for a month. There is nothing easy about explaining that to your ten-, seven-, and four-year-old. Obviously, they were aware that I had a problem. That was plain to see, but having to tell them that I now had to go get help for that problem was very excruciating. Upon hearing that I was going away for a month, they all broke down crying. Kathy was crying, and all three kids were too. Everyone was crying but me. I didn't think I had a problem and honestly thought going to rehab was pointless. The hardest part was watching my kids sobbing, grabbing my pant legs, and not wanting me to go. I will never forget that day. For as selfish and submersed in my own world as I was, that moment still hit me right between the eyes. However, I was emotionless, so it hurts deeper now than it did then.

To soften the blow, Kathy and I decided that we would take a short family trip before they had to drop me off at rehab. The rehab facility was situated in the Texas hill country, so we decided to go spend four days as a family at the Frio River, which was an annual summer trip for us anyway. Instead of taking that time to reassure, comfort, and connect with my family, I used the time as one last soirée. I saw it as my chance to drink as much as I could. Although Kathy had prohibited me from drinking months earlier, she relented, as she knew I was going to do it anyway. After about three days of drinking and isolating at the Frio River, we received a phone call.

Several events had happened along this journey of destruction that should have opened my eyes and snapped me back to reality. This was one of them, but because I was lost and blind to my own unhealthy behavior, I missed the opportunity once again to see the forest for the trees. About 5pm on the second-to-last day of the trip, Kathy got a call on her cell phone from our neighbor, Nancy. She was calling to inform us that we had water coming out of the front door of our home! We quickly shared with our neighbors how to locate the water main and get into our house. They called back and told us that they had shut the water off, but upon going in the house they discovered we had 3-5 inches of water throughout the entire downstairs. This was devastating news. Our lives just went from complicated to officially a mess. Daddy is getting dropped off at rehab, and Momma is left to take care of the kids and a house that has been totally flooded. This was one last chance to turn around, "man up," get my act together, put the bottle down, clean up my life, and go back with my family to handle the cleanup. Instead… I sent a mom back home with three devastated kids to a house that was now unlivable. What a weak excuse of a man I was! Because of my own selfish actions, I was going to rehab and sending my family back to fend for themselves. This was very much a low point in my life. Even though Kathy was adamant that she wanted me to still go get help, I knew this was an opportunity to turn around and do the right thing. Kathy and the kids ended up moving into an extended-stay type hotel (where they would live for the next three months), and I went in to rehab.

Rehab was surreal. It was a place I had never pictured, imagined, or even seen before. After I was processed, the first thing they wanted to do was send me to a detox unit for three or four days. "Detox?" I thought. What in the world is that? They ushered me down to the detox unit, and it was like a hospital. People are on IV's and asleep in hospital beds. It was very eye-opening to say the least! My first reaction was, "No way! I ain't going in there!" I told the nurse, "There's absolutely no way I need to be in detox!" I wanted to leave right then and there, but after consulting with some higher-ups they agreed and placed me in the general population with a roommate.

Remember, I didn't want to be there, was convinced I didn't have a problem. After witnessing the detox unit and all the sedated people strung out on who knows what, I was more convinced than ever that I was just fine. Those people were the ones with the problem. I thought I was going to some type of Alcoholics Anonymous (AA) retreat-like camp and found out in short order it was anything but. I was surrounded by every sort of addiction you can imagine, from crystal meth, heroin, crack, prescription drugs, to alcohol. You name it. There were people from all walks of life, including business executives, teachers, and 18-year-old kids. The fact that I was there felt like a bad dream.

Instead of humbling myself, working the program, and realizing that I was no different than anyone else who was there, I did the exact opposite. I became more arrogant, more belligerent, refused to take part or work any type of program. I considered myself way better and way better off than everyone else, including the instructors. I spent my time working out, making friends with other people who thought this rehab thing was ridiculous, and planning for the day I could get out of there. I went in with my life a mess, and came out with my life in an even bigger disaster.

They allowed one phone call a day, on their phone, and every patient had a family day. On the family day, the relatives of the patient could come up to see the progress and help make amends. I did neither! Very rarely did I make a phone call home, and I invited none of my family to family day.

Twenty-eight days after entering rehab, I was discharged with less than a glowing review from the doctors and staff. What I did next was disgusting. I called home and told them that the rehab was keeping me an extra three days. Then I drove through the gates, went down the hill, stopped at the general store, bought a case of beer, rented a cabin on the river, and drank myself into oblivion for three days. Convinced there was no problem, I was bitter at having been in rehab, and deep down hating myself. I was now in full-blown self-destruction mode.

By that time, my family and friends knew I was a liar. My appearance and attitude told them all they needed to know. "He's no better – he's worse." Consequently, Kathy and I separated. She and the kids were still living at the extended-stay hotel while the house was being repaired, and I lived in the upstairs of our house. This is how it went for close to three months. My family was living at a hotel, and I was at the house drinking every night until I passed out.

We would try to patch things up along the way, but it was a dark time. I was a lying drunk, and my family was limping along without a home, a husband, or a daddy. What a tragedy! I cannot believe how selfish my actions were.

Addiction is so powerful that I can remember at the time being just perfect with the entire setup. I could drink, and no one was around to stop me. In my mind, as warped as it was, the situation was perfect. It was perfect for self-destruction.

Things at work were going south as well. By this time, everyone had caught on to the fact that I was lost, and they were losing me. I didn't have to tell them. It was written all over my actions. Rob, being the loyal friend that he is, did his best to reach me. He made sacrifices, bent over backwards, and literally tried everything to get me to snap out of it. There is not a day that goes by that I don't regret what I put him through. God bless him for sticking by me, even when he should have cut and run.

Kathy, my parents, Rob, my closest friends – everyone was trying to get help for me. I wouldn't listen, though. I would meet with the pastor who was representing the "40 Days to Recovery" program just to appease those around me. I would leave the meeting and go drink. I remember having to attend a meeting in the fall of 2010 with the lead pastor from a big church in town. I will never forget what he told me. It was kind of like the house flooding. It was another sign I should have picked up on, but I didn't. The pastor told me: "You are at a crossroads in your life. You can choose to take the right path or stay down the wrong one. If you do, though, you're headed over the edge." Simple wisdom. Yet another chance to turn around. I heard what he said, but I didn't receive it. It was in one ear, out the other, and on to the next drink.

Somehow, we managed to seemingly pull things back together, and heading into November of 2010, Kathy and the kids moved back into the house. After three long months, the house was now restored from the flood, and Kathy and I took that opportunity to start over. I had my family back and we had our house back. We were determined to use this opportunity as a fresh start. We made it through Thanksgiving, and in early December we were decorating for Christmas one night when I looked at Kathy and said, "I'm so thankful to have you guys and thankful that Rob has stuck by us." Kathy responded, "Yeah, you should really call and thank him." I stopped what I was doing, called Rob to thank him for sticking by us, and apologized for my actions. That moment of gratitude and thanksgiving was short-lived, however. It was a total falsehood because I was still living a lie. I was still self-destructing and now deeper in a web of lies than ever before. My cunningness had reached new heights, as I had to feed an addiction that everyone in my life now knew about.

After Christmas, Kathy and I took the kids, along with some family friends, back to the Frio River to ring in the new year. My family and our friends that were there knew I wasn't supposed to drink, but I did it anyway. I hid it everywhere and even talked them into letting me have a beer or two in front of them. The look on the kids' faces was total disbelief and devastation. I remember riding into town with my buddy, who didn't want me to drink, to buy some beer. He looked over at me and said, "Dude, are you supposed to be doing this? Do you think your family and your team would be okay with this? You just went to rehab." I shot back, "Yeah, they're all fine with it. It's just a beer." That question and answer stick with me to this day.

Upon returning from the Frio River in early January, we still had a few days left until school was set to start. I used that time to isolate, hunt, and drink. The last hunt I was going to go on was January 3, 2011. This was an impromptu hunt that Rob and I decided to take just outside College Station. I should not have gone. I had projects that needed to be done at work and around the house. I looked at these hunts as a chance to get in the woods with a backpack full of alcohol and drown myself where no one could see. I thought I was smart, thought I was hiding it, thought I was masking the smell with gum and Copenhagen snuff, but I wasn't fooling anyone, especially not this day.

Rob was set to pick me up at the house around 4:00pm to make the 30-minute drive to our hunting spot. Rob was taking his son, and we were going to meet the foreman of the ranch out there. Instead of going home, picking up my son and all going together, I left my son at home and brought a backpack full of whiskey and beer. I remember going home to change into my hunting gear, and there right in front of me was my 10-year -old son doing laundry for his mom. I walked right past him, never even asking if he wanted to go, and said, "Daddy's going hunting. I will see you later." What a shame. I should have been helping with the chores and I should have asked him to go. I did neither.

Four hours later, Rob and the ranch foreman found me passed out drunk in my deer stand. There were empty beer cans everywhere, a whiskey bottle, and a loaded rifle in my lap. The gig was up! The lie was over! I passed out before I could cover any of my tracks. It was over!

The next thing I remember was stumbling out of Rob's truck onto my driveway, which led to an argument with my wife with the kids crying in the background. I passed out on the couch and woke up early the next morning not knowing where my truck was. I called Rob as if nothing had happened and asked if he could come pick me up for work, and he said, "Sure."

As Kathy was leaving the house to take the kids to school, she looked at me and said, "Your truck is still at the hunting lease, and you better hope Rob doesn't fire you today." I thought to myself, "No way that's happening."

Rob arrived a few minutes later. He pulled in the driveway and honked the horn. I came out and jumped in the front seat like nothing happened and said, "Mornin,' buddy!" Rob looked at me with heartbreak, disappointment, and disgust in his eyes. He said two simple words I will never forget: "I'm done." With those words, on January 4, 2011, I had officially gone from the top all the way to the bottom, destroyed my family, myself, and broken the heart of my best friend.

Pictured: Kyler (10), me, Kathy, Klaire (7), and Khloe (4) leaving the house to take me to rehab in July of 2010. This truly would be the last time (for a long time) that we took a picture that looked this happy, even though everyone was dying inside. I guess we all still held out hope that rehab would fix me. If only I would have looked at this picture and really understood how much I was breaking these precious hearts. Maybe it would have turned out different. Instead of using rehab to help turn things around and come out a better man, I came out worse and triggered a chain of events that would change our lives forever. This would also be the last time that we would live in this house again for a while, as it completely flooded three days later.

Story #14

Wanting to Die

When I speak and share my testimony with groups, I always say, "Rob Childress didn't fire me. I fired me." For over a year, I was shown grace and given every opportunity to make a change, but I refused. I threw it all away for a life of sin, addiction, lies, and self-absorption. I was now trapped, exposed, living at rock bottom, and wanting to die.

The hardest part of getting fired was telling my family. I waited at the house all day, and when my wife and kids got home, I met them at the door. I told Kathy first, who, probably in shock, didn't act that surprised. I'm sure that she had seen this coming. She simply replied, "I told you this was going to happen! Now what are we going to do?" Then I gathered my three kids upstairs and set out on informing them that daddy was no longer a baseball coach and that I no longer coached at Texas A&M. What I learned from this conversation was and truly is amazing. While I thought the kids would be distraught, they didn't bat an eye. They said they loved me, wanted me to get better, and that they didn't want anything to happen to me, never making one mention of baseball. Seems I was the only one that had my identity tied to baseball.

The next 40 days were a living hell. In a little over a year's time, I had gone from the top of the mountain to butt over tea kettle, all the way down the mountain, and landed with a resounding thud. Gone were my job (which I considered the best assistant coaching job in America), a huge salary, benefits, a free truck, and most importantly the coaches, players, and lots of friends. I spent the next several weeks and months in total shock and agony. I couldn't sleep, couldn't eat, and really couldn't function at all. People from all over were calling, texting, and wanting to know what in the world had happened. I wasn't truthful to any of them. It was miserable. I was trapped by my own selfishness and pride. Our house was put up for sale two weeks later. I was now attending AA meetings every day and a rehab outpatient meeting at night, once a week. So devastated by the fact that I had thrown it all away, I quit drinking once again. It only lasted through February of 2011. I was still lying to myself and living in denial. I was quickly becoming more and more bitter. In order to keep my family intact, I agreed to go to AA every day, and I did for a while. After about a month and a half, I just couldn't take it anymore. While my family would get up each morning and go to school and work, and while the team would convene at the stadium to prepare for the upcoming season, I was at home. I would pace for hours on end hoping, begging, pleading that this was all just a bad dream. Then I would drive across town and attend the AA meetings. I had a sponsor, but I never participated. I resented being there, and I still thought I was better than everyone in the room, even though I was probably the most lost person there! I remember thinking while in the meetings, "I just can't take any more of this. All these people do is complain about their problems. I don't have a problem. Everyone else has the problem." I wanted to die. I thought my world was over. My identity as *Matt Deggs, the baseball man* was gone, all my friends and relationships were seemingly gone, and my family couldn't take me anymore either. It felt as though I had nothing else to live for. I would obsess over the thought of losing it all, then devise ways in my head to end it all, only to return to the thought of losing it all. There was no break in my mind. I couldn't go five minutes without these thoughts racing through my head. The agony was paralyzing. The only thing I can equate it to is if you accidentally killed the person closest to you. In essence, that's exactly what I had done. I had crushed my life, my family, my friends, and my career... but not accidentally. I did it knowingly! It felt like a death. The heartache and grief were torturous and unbearable.

At the height of my despair and desperation, as a last-ditch effort to stay alive, I would sleep next to my five-year-old daughter at night. I held her close, so I could feel her heartbeat. Every day seemed like it lasted 48 hours. The hours on the clock crept by as I would count them down until I could finally fall asleep. Sleep was the only time there was any type of peace, and I absolutely dreaded waking up. Waking up meant you had to face the day all over again while everyone else went to school or to a job. I was left alone with the consequences of my actions.

One day, I decided I couldn't do it anymore. I couldn't do the AA or the outpatient rehab meetings. I was done. The only way out, for me, was to go back to the only thing I knew, alcohol.

After 40 days, gone were the phone calls, the inquiries, and the calls from people checking in on me. I was now left to face myself, and I wasn't brave enough to do it. Even though I had lost everything for the sake of a beer bottle, I went running back to the only thing I thought knew, understood, or loved me...alcohol. Losing my family, my job, many friendships, a huge salary with unbelievable benefits, and literally wanting to die were only enough to keep me from drinking for 40 days. It's unbelievable, but this speaks to the power of addiction. The lies were back. Instead of going to AA, I drank. Instead of going to nightly meetings, I drank. I began to come up with new ways to hide it as well. I welcomed vodka into the picture for the first time because it is colorless and somewhat odorless. I would hide it in water bottles all over the place and thought no one would know.

Just when you think it can't get worse, it always can. Just when you think you have hit rock bottom, you haven't. I was still alive, physically, but I was shackled, chained, and living in a prison of my own making. There was no way out.

Pictured: Me in the spring of 2011. Kathy took this photo of me passed out drunk while sitting up on the edge of our bed. I truly didn't want to live anymore. I had thrown it all away for alcohol and felt like I really didn't have anything left. My identity was gone

with my job in baseball. I was lost and living in a prison of my own making. This is what hopelessness, despair, and addiction look like. Even though I had thrown it all away, I still couldn't quit drinking. Kathy took the picture, I'm sure, in utter disbelief that I was determined to destroy myself and family. She showed it to me the next day, and I didn't know what to say.

Story #15

Moving On

When you think you are indispensable and irreplaceable, you wake up to the cold hard truth that people move on. Life goes on, and nothing is going to stop it. This was a difficult reality to accept. I stopped hearing from people I considered friends. I no longer had daily interaction with people on campus, the coaches, or the team. Acquaintances and peers that once called to visit or check in had disappeared. People I thought I was close to now wanted nothing to do with me. I was finding out the hard way that the same people you step on or over to get to the top are the same ones you pass on the way down. I had been so egotistical and prideful with the way I treated people for so many years, it was easy to see why I would have so few people left that truly wanted to support a guy in my condition. If you would have called me on the phone back then, I would not have called you back. If you heard from me, it was most likely because I wanted something. If you were to text me, I would have responded if it benefited me. If you walked in the office to visit, I was always busy. The long and short of it was that my time was way more important than yours. I was rude, spoke harshly to people, and only built others up if there was something in it for me.

This attitude wasn't reserved for those that I didn't know very well. I treated everyone like this, including my family and the guys I worked with. It's easy to see why I had no network or outside support left. It was a miserable feeling to lose almost every relationship in my life. The only relationship I thought I needed or had left was the one I had with alcohol. Behind the scenes, thank God, there was a core group of people that never let go. I will never forget that they were there the entire time. Even though we would separate again periodically from time to time, I knew Kathy and the kids loved me. My mom and dad never gave up, as well as my sister, Kathy's parents and grandparents, and three of my childhood friends.

Surprisingly enough, the other person that remained in my life was Rob. He would not give up on me. One of the things that kept me going in the early to middle parts of the spring of 2011 was the fact that once a week Rob and I would meet at a local diner. He would buy me breakfast, and we'd visit for a couple of hours before he would go to the stadium. We talked shop as if nothing had happened. He would ask how I was doing, and I would make up some lie. He knew that I was lying, but other than that it was business as usual. For those two hours I felt like I was normal again. I felt like I was worth something, and I felt like I was alive again. However, when it was time to leave the diner, all the pain and agony would come racing back tenfold. On occasion Rob would bring the other assistants, including my good friend that had been hired to take my place. We would all carry on and reminisce of times gone by. It was surreal, peaceful, and agonizing all at the same time. I will never forget that Rob, for almost nine months, took the time out to do this for me. When everyone else jumped ship, there was a handful of people that stuck it out with me. Praise God for that because they helped save my life.

Times weren't getting any easier. Reality was beginning to set in that life was moving on with or without us. Kathy and I were knee-deep in the mounting pressures that had resulted because of my actions. Our house was for sale since we could no longer afford it. I didn't have a vehicle; my buddy that replaced me in my former job was now driving it. Therefore, we had to buy a used truck. We didn't have insurance and were now living off government-funded "COBRA." Our savings were dwindling, and we were now starting to blow through my retirement just to make ends meet. I was in no condition to be employed, not to mention I had never had any other job outside of coaching baseball. By now, you're thinking, *Why in the world didn't he just man up, put the bottle down, and go get a job, any job?* You are exactly right! I wasn't much of a man back then. I was an excuse-making opportunist that only lived for my own glory and destruction. It was sad but true.

Our plan was for me to work on myself, get sober, get my resume together, and look to land another job in baseball once the 2011 season was over. College baseball has turnover at the end of every season, but the hiring is not until the summer. Here we were, in the middle of the spring of 2011, with pressures mounting, no job, and an expectation of me to get myself together. I did everything but that. I never really committed to working on myself. Outpatient meetings and AA only lasted for six weeks before I decided that wasn't for me. I didn't work on reaching out or beginning to network. I was embarrassed, and deep down knew I was living a lie. I spent very little time preparing a resume to be ready to look for another job. What I did do, however, was to continue drinking, work on finding ways to hide it, and basically do whatever it took to feed my addictions.

With little to no concern of what the future held for me or my family, I was only living for myself and the temporary things of this world. I didn't want to live and felt like I had lost everyone and everything. Instead of using that as motivation, I only dug myself and my family into a deeper hole of misery and despair. I had successfully turned our lives into a bad dream.

Pictured L to R: Sean Matus, Donnie Higgs, me, and my dad. Even though I had been fired, I threw out the first pitch of the season for the Texas City Little League that day in the spring of 2011. I remember being embarrassed, not feeling worthy of taking part in such a special day. Twenty-seven years earlier, the three of us stood on that same field and celebrated a City Championship as 12-year-olds, with my dad as one of the coaches. Even though I had lost contact with most of my friends, peers, and acquaintances, these three guys never let go. They stood by me through every bit of ugliness and never wavered. Donnie and Sean are true brothers, and my dad will always be my hero and best friend. Without these guys, I wouldn't be writing this story today.

Story #16

Living a Nightmare

In late spring 2011, I was addicted, the house was for sale, and no one – I mean no one – was interested in buying it. Our savings were gone, my retirement was dwindling fast, credit cards were getting close to the max, and nothing had changed. Kathy was working hard at the kids' private school to do her best to bring home a little something. The kids were putting on brave faces every day as they went to school, and they still continued making straight A's. They are incredible kids! Everyone was holding up to their end of the bargain… except for me. Kathy had seen enough. By this time, I was in and out of the house. Still living a life of sin, selfishness, and addiction, Kathy and the kids couldn't take it anymore. I was now going back and forth from living in College Station to having to live with my parents in Texas City. I was "ping-ponging" back and forth, staying in one spot until I wore out my welcome, which didn't take long. I realize now how dangerously close I was to losing everyone.

In addition to the obvious hardships we were battling, Kathy's grandpa had taken ill with congestive heart failure. To make matters even worse for her and the kids, they were now on the verge of losing the patriarch of her family. An unbelievably kind and generous human being that everyone loved being around, he was now fighting for his life. With everything I was putting my family through, for them to have to walk through this at the same time had to be unbearable. She was and still is the strongest, most loyal woman I know. It's still hard for me to believe what I subjected her to. I put her through such a torturous nightmare! At the end of May that year, her grandpa passed on.

On the heels of Kathy's grandfather passing, I faced one of the most humbling and agonizing experiences I have ever had to go through. I was having to watch, not actively participate in, but watch the 2011 Texas A&M baseball team absolutely crush it! When I say, "crush it," I mean they were having an incredible season. I can't put into words how difficult this was for me. I know God was humbling me. He had stripped me of everything, and with the love of a Father, he was totally humbling me for my own good.

I watched the Aggies on television from my parents' sofa (because I was kicked out of my house). I watched a team that I had helped recruit, assemble, and coach go on to win the Big 12 Conference regular season title, the Big 12 tournament title, host and win a regional, go on the road to Florida State, win a super regional, and finally break through the gates of Omaha. You want to talk about a kick in the gut! Here I was, a 39-year-old drunk, living with my parents as I watched all of this unfold from a distance. I thought I was "the man" – no way could they do any of this without me, but guess what? They did! This painful lesson drove home the reality that as a coach, it's not about you. The team is going to win with or without you, period. That's the very first thing you better understand.

Of all the consequences I was experiencing during that time, without a doubt that was one of the toughest I had to endure. I will never forget the feeling of not having a home, and then watching a team that I should have been a part of have an amazing season without me. When I was there, we came close in 2007 and 2008, but now they had made it! Even though I was happy for the team and coaches, a huge piece of me was dying inside. I had no one to blame but myself. Like my dad told me, if I had never decided to drink, I would have been there. I did and that's why I wasn't. Simple, but very true.

It wasn't the championships or even the games that I was missing the most. What I was heartbroken over and truly missing were the relationships. I was fast realizing that the relationships are what keep you going. Nothing about baseball was I truly missing. Yes, I loved to compete, but what I was really missing was the time spent in relationship. The conversations, the talks in the office, the bus rides, and laughing in the dugout. When all of that is gone, you have nothing. You will miss the games, but there is no way to replace the relationships. The most painful part for me was in realizing that no one took this from me. I took it from myself. Months after they got back from Omaha, Rob called me on a Saturday morning and invited me to breakfast. When he sat down, he handed me a box. I opened it, and right in front of me was a championship ring with my name on it. For him to do that, after everything I put him through, speaks volumes to his character. I will never forget that.

Pictured: Me and a 10-year-old Kyler, in the late spring of 2011. I had been kicked out of the house and was living in Texas City. Kyler came to visit me for the weekend, and we went to one of my favorite places growing up, the Texas City Dike. A picture really can say a thousand words. I'm lost and Kyler is looking at me as if to say, "Daddy, please come back." Even though they were right in front of me the entire time, I couldn't have been any further from my family. I was lost, and we truly were living a nightmare of my own making.

Chapter 5
Damaged Goods

*Amazing Grace – through the sun and down through the
sand
Amazing Grace – in a barren, desert wasteland.*

*A tree long forgotten & withered in the storm...
Lost, hopeless, broken, and torn.*

*Left to die in a land so harsh, no man dare to pass
Only a miracle could save this life, and that's when God
commanded:
Stand and hold fast.*

*I am doing something new, God roared through the raging
fire of the sun...
You shall be restored, renewed, redeemed; by My grace
we will be as one.*

*You will be deeply rooted when you seek the knowledge
of my character & this shall hold you in your place.
Wisdom, patience, humility, strength, perseverance, all are
found in the Living Water just under the clay.*

*Your trunk shall stand unyielding as a sign of your
confidence, obedience, and faith...
Right next to the stream of tears, as a reminder that I have
wiped them from your face.
By the blinding radiance of My face, your fronds will
blossom, only to reveal My majestic glory*

People from all walks will look up at you in wonder; how did he get here, and what is his story?

You shall answer, "Only by God's amazing grace, through the gift of His Son, do I stand…
He makes ALL things new, even in a barren, desert wasteland."
~ The Vision
June 2011
Matt Deggs

Story #17

The Vision

Something was going on in June 2011. Something was different. Something was changing. I could sense God's presence in my life again. Maybe it was because I was busy updating my resume and applying for jobs. Maybe I was now realizing the urgency to pull it all together and land another job. I decided, once again, to quit drinking.

As hard as the spring had been, somehow we were still here and still standing. I was back living at home, and the end of the baseball season had brought with it a renewed sense of hope and energy as I knew job openings were just right around the corner. I just knew I would land a job, we would sell the house, and start all over somewhere. I didn't know where, but I knew God had something special in store for me and my family. By this time, I was starting to establish somewhat of a routine. I was getting up early again, reading my Bible, working on my resume, filling out applications, securing transcripts and letters of recommendation, and even starting to exercise again. I thought I had seen the error of my ways and was now good to go. "No problem," I thought. "I'm

Matt Deggs. Somebody, somewhere, will be eager to hire me." As the jobs started coming open, I began applying. Initially, I was very picky and selective. "No way I'm applying for that job," is what I said to my wife and my dad about several schools that had openings. I was only applying for the "big jobs." I mean, I was the associate head coach at Texas A&M, and they just got back from the College World Series. Surely someone will notice and give me another chance.

After a couple of weeks of pouring everything I had into the job search, I was quickly beginning to realize that this was going to be a lot harder than I anticipated. No follow-ups, no return phone calls, no return e-mails clued me in that no one was interested in what I was selling. The college baseball world was alive and well and perfectly fine without me. Nobody fully understood why I left A&M so abruptly. Questions abounded and quite frankly, I was a risk that nobody was willing to take.

It was beginning to wear on me, but I remained strong. As the weeks passed, I didn't drink, was reinvesting in my family, and doing my best to stay in the Word of God. I continued to press on, seemingly more determined than ever to get back into "the game," but things just weren't right. I wanted to drink so badly I could taste it. I was dying to go back to my former ways, but I knew in the back of my mind I couldn't, not now at least. I believe I was in the bargaining stage of the grieving process. Essentially, I was making a deal with God. It went something like, "If I lay all the lies, lust, addiction, sin, and arrogance down right now, will You please open a door for me to get back in?" I knew it was a temporary arrangement because my heart truly hadn't changed. I am more than certain that God knew it as well. I think God takes notice, not so much of our actions, but more so of the condition of our heart. My heart was not only broken and shattered, but it was also dark and full of opportunism.

After having my hopes up for another job just to have them dashed again, one day I decided to go lie down on the bed and take a nap to escape from the reality of the situation. I was in a semi-conscious state after lying there about 20 minutes. I was almost asleep but still awake when God spoke a vision into my heart. He showed me an incredible picture of my current state and condition. The vision was like a semi-conscious dream. It was a vibrant look into the future. I saw an open marketplace full of beautiful plants for sale. As I looked around, I noticed, in a perfect straight row, four of the most beautiful queen palms you have ever seen. They were mature, complete, and lacked nothing. They were all planted in beautiful planters and were brilliant and full of life. People were gathered around checking out the prices, choosing one, and buying them up as fast as they could. At the end of the row, however, was one lonely palm. This one was anything but healthy. It was brown, withered, slumped over, and hardly had a hint of green to it at all. Instantly, God spoke to my heart: "You see all those beautiful palms over there? Everyone is going to buy them, but do you see that palm at the end that is dying? That one is you right now. No one is going to buy you right now, in your current condition, but guess what? One day they will!"

I immediately got out of bed, startled by the vision in my head. I was hopeful, yet heartbroken at what the Lord had shared with me. I felt like the last Christmas tree in the "lot." You know, the one that is brownish-green and short that everyone makes fun of or only buys as a joke. Not long after that, I was reading the book of Job in the Bible. To affirm the vision that God had placed on my heart, He led me to a passage I had never come across before.

Job 8:5-7

*But if you will seek God earnestly
and plead with the Almighty,
if you are pure and upright,
even now He will rouse himself on your behalf
and restore you to your prosperous state.
Your beginnings will seem humble,
so prosperous will your future be.*

It wouldn't occur to me until years later that on that summer day back in 2011, God was pleading with me to stay in the fight, take action, and turn things around; and if I did these things, He would take care of the rest. I was too busy worrying about being the ugly Christmas tree to hear His voice. I was blinded by my own personal agenda. It seemed that every door was closed, no one was interested, and no one wanted to purchase a withering palm.

Pictured: Although not much of an artist, I went immediately after God had shown me the vision and drew what was in my heart. I wrote a poem correlating with what I saw called, "The Vision." This happened three times that summer. I wrote and drew after each one of them. I made myself a promise that if I ever got back into baseball, this collection of poems and drawings would always be in my office. If you ever stop by, you will find them all on a shelf right across from my desk.

Story #18

From the Bulldogs to the Jackrabbits

As the summer wore on, I was still unemployed but still not drinking. It was a miracle that I had held out for over a month. Even after the vision that God had put on my heart, I pressed on in my search to get back into baseball. My confidence by this point was waning, but I was still undeterred and undaunted. I was still sure of my ability and certain of the fact that someone would hire me. I was also still convinced that I didn't have a problem. I was in an obvious "bargaining" phase. Even if someone hired me, I knew in the back of my mind, I was going to drink again. In fact, I couldn't wait for that day! The only thing that had really changed was the fact that now I wasn't so picky when looking for jobs. I had evolved from only looking for jobs that I felt were "worthy" of me to applying for anything that came open, from the Texarkana Junior College "Bulldogs" to the South Dakota State "Jackrabbits."

It wasn't like there weren't opportunities. It felt like a million jobs came open that summer. A new job came open almost every day, at every level of baseball, and I applied for all of them! By this point, I was an expert at filling out applications and writing cover letters, but all to no avail. I ran through the entire gamut of baseball jobs including the SEC, NAIA, junior colleges, high schools, and even the professional ranks, only to have the door closed in my face every time. For three months the door would crack open, I would do my best to get through it, and then right before I got in, it would seemingly slam shut. There were some close calls, but mostly just very humbling experiences. Looking back, I had no shot; nor was I in any shape or condition to coach and mentor young men. I am very thankful I wasn't hired because that would have, at some point, marked the end of my career officially!

I had a phone interview with Ole Miss and the same with Arizona. Both were for assistant coaching jobs. I had a phone interview with Southern Illinois for their head coach position, and I even flew to South Dakota and interviewed in person with South Dakota State for their head coaching job. Florida International and the University of Central Florida also needed assistants. I can remember trying to talk Turtle Thomas, head coach at Florida International at that time, into letting me coach the pitchers because he needed a pitching coach. I had never coached pitchers and was a hitting coach by trade. The Sam Houston State University head coaching job came open, and I did a phone interview with the athletic director, Bobby Williams. They wisely hired David Pierce from Rice University instead. I can remember thinking the "SHSU" job would be a perfect fit because they were only 45 minutes away from College Station. I even called David Pierce after he got the job to see if he needed an assistant, but he already had his guys in place. I sent resumes to the University of Nebraska and the University of Tennessee because they had openings. Obviously, I heard nothing back. I was living in my own personal dream world. East Tennessee State and Northwestern State University both had assistant coach openings, but I couldn't get in the door at either school. I was quickly running out of options. Ironically, Texarkana Junior College, the school where I had spent five years as the head coach and had arguably the best five-year run of anyone that had ever coached there, had a vacancy for their head coaching post. I applied, made phone calls, reached out, and … nothing. I helped guide them to their first-ever Junior College World Series appearance, and did not even get a return phone call? That should tell you all you need to know! I was damaged goods, yesterday's news. Years of fulfilling my own agenda and living for my own personal gain had now caught up with me. Talk about humiliated and humbled, that was me. At least, it should have been. Instead of taking this as my cue to change, I took it as a personal slight as I carried on thinking everyone had a problem except me.

Heading into late July, I was now at the end of my rope. Job openings were slowing to a trickle, and the ones that had come open were filled quickly. I was going to give it until the end of August, and then I was going to have no choice but to suck it up, move on, and find a real job. About that time, the Galveston College head coaching job came open. Galveston College is a junior college 15 minutes from where Kathy and I grew up. "GC" Baseball, once upon a time, had experienced an incredible run of success. They even won a national championship. The same day the Galveston College job opened, my mom sent me a Bible verse. It was Revelation 3:7-8: *What he opens no one can shut, and what he shuts no one can open. I know your deeds. See, I have placed before you an open door that no one can shut. I know that you have little strength, yet you have kept my word and have not denied my name.* Being in the "bargaining" phase, I took this as a sign, so, I quickly tracked down the GC athletic director's name and phone number. A week later, I found myself sitting in a room with all the administrators from Galveston College. I was convinced this was it. Kathy and I would move the family back home, and we would start all over at Galveston College. I interviewed for the job as hard as I could that day. I was fighting for my baseball life. I looked at this as my last chance. I had made binders for everyone, bought a new suit, and gave it everything I had for eight hours. Afterwards, I thought I had it in the bag. I could already see the headline: "Former A&M assistant coach and Galveston County boy comes back home." Man, was I ever presumptive, egotistical, and full of myself! The only problem was, Galveston College had other plans. They hired someone else more deserving and better prepared. They hired the right man for the job. I read the verse my mom had sent that day as if God had "opened" a door, but the way it was intended to be read was that He actually "closed" a door that no man can open.

Back to the whole "vision" thing. It would be a long, long time before any door in baseball would be opened again. It's a feeling that is hard to eloquently put into words; to have a perception of yourself that no one sees but you. Is it narcissism, or is it just arrogance and ego? I'm not sure. I just knew my resume was as good or better than anyone I was going up against, but no one else seemed to see it that way. My identity was crushed, my confidence was running on fumes, and I was faced with the fact that no one wanted me. The good news was that, somehow, I was now without a drink for over two months. However, I was only doing what had to be done. There was no permanence in my commitment. I was, what they call in AA, "white-knuckling" my way through it.

Pictured: My grandpa, Rock Giddings, and me in 2001. My grandpa was my best friend growing up and the man I most wanted to be

like. Although he never got to see me coach many games, he did show up for this one. This pic was taken after the 2001 Texarkana College Bulldogs won the Region XIV tournament and advanced to the Junior College World Series in Grand Junction, Colorado, for the first time in school history. I could not have been any prouder that my grandpa was there to share that moment. Even though we had tremendous success on and off the field, just 10 years later I would be looking for a job and wouldn't get a return phone call from them. It still stings a little. I don't blame them. I was in no condition to coach or lead anyone, and I'm thankful that they passed on me. The following year, TC closed its baseball program altogether due to a lack of funding. Sometimes when we think a prayer goes unanswered, it really has been answered. We just don't know it yet. Had we packed up and moved back to Texarkana, I would have been jobless again in a year.

Story #19

Feed Mill at 40

One last job came open in middle of August 2011 at a small, private NAIA school located in downtown Nashville, Tennessee. Trevecca Nazarene University needed a new baseball coach. After mulling it over for a day or two, I decided to toss my name in the hat. I was doing my absolute best to humble myself and try to have perspective, although I wasn't very good at it. I convinced myself that I was the right man for the job and that I would have no problem moving my family to Nashville, no matter what the job paid. I filled out the application, made a couple of phone calls, and found myself taking part in a two-hour phone interview with the new AD and the president of the university. The phone interview went well enough that they invited me up for a formal interview the following week, so Kathy and I drove from College Station to Nashville. The interview went on over the course of two days. Once again, I was prepared and fought for that job with everything I had. I knew for a fact that, for at least a year, this would be it. I thought if I sat out another year, I would likely never coach again at the college level. I was as open and honest as I could be, but never truly forthcoming as to why I was unemployed. I thought the interview went great, and once again I was somewhat confident that this would be the one. Kathy and I would load up the family, move to Nashville, and start over in the NAIA to work our way back up to where we were.

A week later, as I waited on pins and needles, the phone finally rang. I answered, and it was the AD from Trevecca Nazarene. We made the usual small talk for five minutes or so, the kind where you get the vibe that what's coming is not what you want to hear. He finally got to the point and explained that he was going to go with somebody else. I then proceeded to unload eight months of anger and frustration on him. Yep, I did something I had been known to do many times over the years when things didn't go my way. I proceeded to verbally assault this man over the phone and informed him in no uncertain terms that he had wasted my time and chosen the wrong man for the job. I asked him what I was supposed to do now, and before hanging up I even accused him of putting an end to my career. Unbelievable! I still can't believe I used to act like that, on a regular basis. It's no wonder I was unemployed!

The first thing I wanted to do was drink, but for some unknown reason I didn't. It's a good thing because at that point, I think I would have truly unraveled. We were now at a definite crossroads. I was out of options. Every door had slammed shut and the window of opportunity was gone. Approaching my 40th birthday, here I was, unemployed, broke, and hopeless. I had no idea what to do next! To make matters far worse, we were still living in College Station, our house wouldn't sell, the kids were having to change schools from private to public, Kathy was going to have to find another job, and we had now blown through all our money. I had assumed that we would find another job in the summer of 2011, the house would sell, and we would pick up and start all over. None of that happened! It was gut-wrenching to watch my kids have to change schools because of me. It was more gut-wrenching to sit them down and explain that they were now on free lunch. It was killing me that Kathy had to go find another job to help support us, while I had nothing. Watching as the kids had to leave all their friends behind and go start all over at a new school just added to the pain. All of this because of me and my actions – no one else but me!

I now had to do something, and fast, but had absolutely no clue what I was going to do next. There was nothing else I knew or was interested in. I applied for the Texas state troopers, but I was 39 about to be 40. I looked at teaching classes at a community college since I have a master's degree in education. I applied to high schools just to teach and not coach, but now was not the time for a career change. I just needed a job, any job, and needed one soon. We were not going to be able to make ends meet for another two weeks. We weren't sinking anymore. We were sunk! I swallowed my pride and reached out to a man that I had come to know over the past couple of years. He owned a feed mill about 15-20 miles outside of College Station. We sat down and talked. He knew a little about our situation but not all of it. I explained how desperate we were at this point, and he agreed to help us out and put me to work. The day after I turned 40, I went to work at a feed mill making much less than even 1/4 of my former salary.

I was the logistics coordinator for the incoming and outgoing 18-wheelers that were hauling feed from one place to another. Even though I knew nothing of logistics coordination or the feed business, I jumped in and tried to figure it out the best I could. The days felt treacherously long. I would get there at 7am and leave at 5pm. I was used to having a job where the days seemed to fly by and there were never enough hours in the day. Now I was in a job that felt like the day crept along at a snail's pace. Coordinating logistics didn't take much of my day. Mostly, I swept the floors and loaded 18-wheelers full of cattle feed, horse feed, and deer corn. This was manual, back-breaking work with guys from Mexico and Guatemala. Although we didn't speak the same language, it was a bright spot getting to work alongside those men. They worked incredibly hard and getting to know them, they all had amazing stories. The hardest part for me was dealing with the dust which flared up my asthma and allergies. If you have never been in a feed mill, it's so dusty that it looks smoky. I would have to wear a mask to avoid coughing and sneezing all day. I would go to the mill feeling fine every morning and come home with what felt like a sinus infection every evening, but I finally had some semblance of worth and value again. I finally felt like I was needed again. My family was proud of me for taking the job and working so hard at something so laborious that I knew nothing about. I had been sober for over three months. I will forever be grateful to Matt Moore and his family for hiring me at the feed mill and giving me an opportunity to work when no one else would.

In a final kick in the gut, after being on the job for about three weeks, my phone rang while I was loading a pallet full of cattle feed. I recognized the number. It was Turtle Thomas, the head coach at Florida International University in Miami. A couple of months earlier, I had tried to talk him into hiring me as his pitching coach, but never heard back. I answered as fast as I could, praying that he was calling to offer me a job. After the initial "small talk," he informed me that he was just calling to let me know that he hired someone else. I said thanks, hung up, chuckled to myself in disbelief, and went back to slinging cattle feed on a pallet. I honestly didn't know how much longer I could keep this up. I was bitter, angry, full of resentment, and white-knuckling my way through sobriety. I had fallen so very far and I could not get over how I allowed this to happen. It was eating at me from the inside out.

Driver	Truck/Load	Prdct/Qnty	Customer	Dest.	Cust. Cont.	Cell #	Del. Due	Actual Del.	Notes

Pictured: Ever the coach, this is a copy of a chart that I made while coordinating 18-wheeler logistics at the feed mill. Even though I had no clue what I was doing, I still wanted to figure out a way to efficiently and effectively get the job done. That's just the way my mind has always worked. If I'm going to do something, I want to get the job done and win. I created this chart at home. I still have it to remind me of how fragile life is, and even when you're at the top, you are never truly that far from the bottom. Things like this keep me grounded and humble.

Story #20

Drug Dealer

Now back in somewhat of a routine after eight months of turmoil, everyone in the family had somewhere to be and something to be responsible for each morning. The kids started their new schools and were doing their best to adjust to having new surroundings and new classmates. Kathy began a new job at a local preschool and I was reporting to the feed mill each morning. The situation was not ideal, but we were, at least, in somewhat of a routine again. I was going on four months sober, and the family was still intact. As dark as those times were, we were far better off than we had been just months earlier. The house, however, was still on the market with no offers. Even though we were both working again, we were hemorrhaging financially. We had way more going out than what we had coming in, and it was only a matter of time before we lost the house. This was a product of living well beyond our means even when I was coaching.

The feed mill had helped to restore some type of normalcy and add a little income, but there was no way we could afford to make this permanent. There was just not enough money for the amount of work and no way I could continue to come home sick every day. I decided to reach out to my old friend Jeremy Talbot who coached with me at A&M until he moved his family back to South Louisiana. JT was working for a pharmaceutical company and had become very successful at it. In an act of total desperation, I called JT and asked if they were hiring. I remember him being very reluctant. He told me in a roundabout way that the money can be good but the job can be demanding and tough. "You better make real sure this is what you want to do because this job will eat you alive if you're not serious about it," he said. I went on to tell him that essentially I had no choice. The house wasn't selling and I was out of moves. In a matter of a month or two it was going to be checkmate. This job would be the closest thing I could find to try to recoup my salary. JT made a phone call or two, and before I knew it, I was sitting down for an in-person interview with representatives from Forest Pharmaceuticals. I remember mapping out my career for them, and the one area they were really interested in was learning about *The Pack* and *The Pack Mentality*. This intrigued them, and it was the first time that it dawned on me that *The Pack* transcends baseball. It is a model for all organizations. It helped that the guy I met with is a former athlete. I thought after the interview they would let me know something, but apparently that's not the way it works in big business. I had a second interview in a room at Bush Intercontinental Airport and then went on an all-day ride-along. The hardest question I have ever been asked occurred during my second interview. The VP of the division asked me point blank, "Are you done with baseball? If not, we cannot invest our time in you." I will never forget having to answer that question. I looked him right in the eye and lied right to his face: "Yes sir, I'm done. That life is in the past for me. I'm ready for something else." That's the hardest answer I have ever given, and I prayed to God that it wasn't true.

Still working at the feed mill, I finally got a phone call one afternoon. It was Forest Pharmaceuticals, and they were calling to offer me a job. I said yes immediately and informed Matt Moore, the owner of the feed mill. I thanked him and told him how much I was indebted to him but that I needed to make more money to support my family. Next, I called JT to tell him thanks for being such a good friend and helping me out in my time of need. This would not be the last time I would need JT to do me a life-changing favor. I should have held off a little before resigning from the feed mill. I quickly found out in the coming days that even though Forest hired me, I really didn't have the job yet. I had to pass three weeks of what they call "in-home" school training before I could move on to New York City, where they would train me for three more weeks. Only if I passed all of that would I have the job.

Still sober, and now very determined, I attacked the three-week home school course with everything I had. This was, to date, the most pressure-packed assignment I had ever taken on. The deal was, you studied all day on your computer at home and then took a test every evening. This went on every day and night for three weeks. I was working close to 15 hours a day on this stuff. There were two caveats: 1) If you didn't complete the program in time, you didn't get the job, and 2) If you failed even one test, you didn't get the job. I was scared to death! It was like having to learn a completely new and different language in three weeks. I had never studied that hard in my life. I was responsible for learning as much as I could about three different drugs: 1) Bystolic (a blood pressure medicine), 2) Daliresp (a Chronic Obstructive Pulmonary Disease drug), and 3) Namenda (an Alzheimer's medicine). These would be the three drugs that I would be responsible for and my territory was set to be southeast Texas. Close, but still two hours away from College Station. I would, ironically enough, cover Texas City to Pasadena and everything in between. First, I was going to have to make it through home school and New York training. I closed my eyes, hit *submit*, and thankfully passed my last home school test. I have no clue how, but I did it! Desperation is a funny motivator. It can drive people to crazy feats they never thought possible.

It was now the first part of October and my next step would be three weeks of on-campus training in New York City. I left for NYC on October 10 and would not return until October 28. Now going on my fifth month without a drink, this would be my first big test. I had never been to New York and didn't know any of my classmates, but I was open-minded and desperate to jump these hurdles so I could begin the job. The training was unbelievably grueling! They housed us at a nice hotel, we ate well, and they had a place to work out; but that's about where the good time would begin and end. We caught a bus every morning, rode the 20 minutes to their training facility, and attended class after class after class all day for three weeks. Like home school, they taught and then we had to test or present.... Either way it was pass or fail, and fail was not acceptable.

I'm thankful for this time in my life. I made some great friends, learned many valuable business and selling lessons, and was challenged in a way that I had never been before in an arena I knew nothing about. Somehow, after three weeks, I didn't just survive; I thrived. At the end of the three weeks they presented awards for most outstanding achievement in each of the three drugs that we would be selling. I was awarded the most outstanding student for two of the three. For the first time in history, a student had won more than one award, and that student was me. I couldn't believe it. That was the good news. The bad news was that one night, after having been there about two weeks, I decided to have some wine with dinner while out with my classmates. They had no clue about me, and I thought, "What could a little wine hurt?" Five months down the drain! Although I excelled in the classroom, I once again had failed outside of it, letting not only myself down, but my family who was counting on me. I made a promise to myself that I wouldn't do it again. A week later with training now complete, I was at the airport bar sucking down beers while waiting on my flight back to Texas.

The commute from College Station to my territory in Southeast Houston was a grind, to say the least. It was two hours there and two hours back every day. To break up the trip after work, I would stop at a restaurant or bar and drink. Sadly, I was on the way back to being a drunk and a liar once more. Even though I had excelled in training, I quickly realized I was terrible at the job. I didn't want to do this job and felt like a fish out of water. Baseball was all I ever knew or wanted to know. I was now missing it more than ever and spent all my time either drinking, selling pharmaceuticals, or praying to God to open another door in baseball come the spring. Drinking and praying is an oxymoron, but I was great at it. Baseball jobs never come open in the spring. It's always the summer, but I was still holding out the slightest bit of hope. During the months of November, December, and January I would stay at my parent's house three or four nights during the week and go home to College Station on the weekends to ease the commute. Once again, I was a man without a home, becoming more and more lost, and starting to lose all hope. During the weeks in Texas City, I would go buy beer after work, sit on the Texas City Dike, and drink it all as I watched the ships pass by. I was in a dark place again and totally consumed with times gone by. I was yearning once more for things to go back to the way they were. Inevitably, reality would snap me to, the alarm clock would go off the next morning, and I would start the same routine all over again. On the weekends in College Station, I would have to white-knuckle my way through without a drink or lie and say I had to go somewhere, then slip off for a drink. No matter where I was, my thoughts always went back to the same thing: "It's over, I can't stop drinking, I hate my job, I'm never getting back into baseball, and I have ruined everything." It's hard to admit, but I was hopeless and more than ever wanting to die. I went from it being a passing thought to picturing ways to do it. I didn't think I could go on, and I was beginning to believe that everyone would honestly be better off without me.

Then… just like that, it happened! A February day in 2012 I will never forget. God gave me a ray of light through a little crack. I was finishing up my day at a doctor's office. Actually, I was finishing up my day by getting yelled at by a doctor. That was the thing about selling pharmaceuticals; you better be thick-skinned because you often got treated like a second-class citizen with very little respect. It just depended on what type of day the doctor and staff were having. This was totally foreign to me. I was used to being the center of attention, and now nobody cared a thing about who I was. This was yet another reason I was totally fed up. I strolled out of the office glad it was time to end the day. I couldn't wait to get to the convenience store to buy a six-pack of "tall boys." That's when it happened. Shortly after making my way to the store, my phone rang. It was JT. He said: "Dude, you are never going to believe this, but UL (University of Louisiana) is losing their hitting coach/recruiting coordinator. Nobody knows, but he is taking a different job outside of baseball and leaving in a week or so." I said excitedly, "Call them right now and tell them I will go there for free." What happened next still amazes me. Even though God had opened a door of hope, I hung up, marched right in the convenience store, and bought the six-pack. I proceeded to drink it all, then prayed all night that God would bless me with the job. Hard to fathom, I know, but that's what I did. I was the least-deserving person to be blessed with that job.

Three days later, Coach Robichaux, the head coach at UL, called. We talked and agreed to meet. Almost dead, and now I had a heartbeat.

Pictured: An instructor at the Forest Pharmaceutical training facility in New York and me in October of 2011. I should have been in fall baseball practice somewhere, but instead I spent an agonizing three weeks in home school training and another three weeks training in NYC. Although I stood out in the classroom and in training, I also began another death spiral by deciding to drink again.

Pictured: My briefcase and two of the products I was selling. One of the hardest parts of the job, for me, was the waiting. I am very impatient by nature, and it was not uncommon to sit for over an hour in the lobby waiting to get a meeting with the doctor. I took this picture and kept it, to remind me that I never want to go back to be the person I once was. There is absolutely nothing wrong with selling pharmaceuticals. It's a great job, if you can land it. It just wasn't for me. I was a fish out of water and, quite frankly, I was terrible at it.

Pictured: A random ship passing through the Texas City ship channel one afternoon in the fall of 2011. I would sometimes take pictures of ships passing by while I sat and drank my life away. I don't know why I took the pictures or was so drawn to sitting on the Dike and watching the ships, but I was. It was there that I would often ask myself if I truly wanted to go on.

Chapter 6
Breaking Free

Each of you should use whatever gift you have received to serve others, as faithful stewards of God's grace in its various forms.
~ 1 Peter 4:10

Story #21

430 Days

God's grace truly is greater than our sin. I, undoubtedly, had done nothing to deserve the opportunity that was now before me. Nevertheless, here I was, face to face with Coach Tony Robichaux of the University of Louisiana Ragin' Cajuns. It was Saturday, February 18, 2012; and it was cold and rainy in San Marcos, Texas. Coach Robe and I didn't seem to mind. He was looking for a hitting coach and recruiting coordinator, and I was just looking to get back into baseball. This was the first time I had ever had a conversation with Coach Robe. Sure, we knew of each other and we were always cordial, but we certainly weren't friends nor had we ever run in the same circles.

We sat in a back room of the Holiday Inn for what seemed like three or four hours that morning and talked about everything, not just baseball. I shared my story, and he told me that all of that was in the past and that he was a man that believed in second chances. He told me the only thing that mattered now was what I did moving forward. He said, "I don't care what you've done. I care about what you're going to do." I had never had anyone talk to me with such wisdom and grace. I remember thinking that this was a "God" thing and I was literally sitting there praying that Coach Robe would hire me for the job.

Shocking to me, he started talking about *The Pack* and *The Pack* offense and mentality. I was like "What?" I was blown away because I was sure that he knew nothing of *The Pack*. He then went on to explain, saying, "Remember when y'all beat us in the championship game of the regional in 2007?" I said, "Yeah, why?" He continued, "We were in your team's dugout and had access to the clubhouse." In suspense, I said, "Go on..." Then Coach Robe went on to tell me that he went in there and studied all our *Pack* handouts that were hanging in the clubhouse. "I have been intrigued by it for the last five years," he said. Wow! Then he said, "Now I have a chance to get the guy that built *The Pack* and that's what I want to do. The job is yours if you want it." Crazily, I told Coach Robe that I would have to talk to Kathy and work on finding a place to live, as our house still hadn't sold and it was the middle of the school year and there was just a lot to figure out.

I was scared to death telling Coach Robe those things, but it was the truth. Thankfully, Coach Robe is a very patient, understanding, and fair man. He simply said, "Take your time." I thanked him, got up, got in the truck, and drove as fast as I could towards College Station. As happy as I was on the drive back, all I kept telling myself was, "Don't drink. Just don't stop, don't drink..." I wanted to stop at the store, buy some beer, and celebrate so badly I could taste it. I even stopped, went inside a convenience store, looked around, circled the beer cooler twice, but ultimately summoned the courage and left. How could I? How could I stop and drink after God had just poured His Grace out on me and given me an open door full of so much hope? I stayed strong and finally made it to the house.

I talked with Kathy, and we both agreed that we had no clue as to how we were going to make this work; but like she said, "You've got to do it." The next day, I called Coach Robe and took the job. I will never forget his response when I informed him I was taking the job. He simply said, "Okay," and that was it. Not, "Happy to have you," "Congrats," or "I can't wait to get started." He just said, "Okay." I remember being alarmed at the time, but as I would soon learn, that's just Coach Robe. That's one of the many things I love about him. He takes his time, he's measured, he's thought out, he is patient, and he never gets too excited. God knew exactly what I needed, even if I didn't, and Coach Robe was just the man for the job. Coach Robe quickly became more than a boss; in no time he turned into a big brother, loyal friend, confidant, and mentor. God, on the other hand, must have a big-time sense of humor because he had just taken a drunk and placed him in Lafayette, Louisiana – the undisputed drinking capital of the US.

It would be another three weeks before I would reach Lafayette. The team was now 13 games into the season, and I was chomping at the bit to get started. The time had finally arrived. On March 9, 2012, I coached in my first game at UL. It was a 12-5 victory over Southern Mississippi University. Four hundred thirty days after getting fired, I was now back in the game I loved. I thought it was never going to happen, but it did. I couldn't help but get emotional during that first National Anthem thinking of all the prayers I had thrown up to God, begging Him to open the door that spring (something that never happened). Lo and behold, here I was. God is faithful, even if we don't deserve it. Thank you, Lord.

That first season at UL was anything but smooth. Don't get me wrong, I was thankful for the second chance and more than happy to be there, but I was met with some serious challenges from the get-go. In other words, I had my work cut out for me. It was going to be an uphill battle to get back on my feet, and it was not going to be easy.

I soon learned that the Cajun culture is one big family. Not having a place to live, the Cajuns' associate head coach, Anthony "Babs" Babineaux, and his wife Joni welcomed me into their home. That's the way it works down there. If someone is in need, then everyone pitches in. For the next three and a half months, I would be, yet again, separated from my family. Since our house hadn't sold and it was the middle of the school year, Kathy and I decided it would be best for them to stay put. I lived in the Babineaux's guest room for the remainder of the 2012 season. They made me feel like family and certainly always welcomed my family when they visited. I will always be indebted to Babs and Joni for their hospitality.

The 2012 UL team was young, inexperienced, not very deep and lacked leadership. Understanding this, Coach Robe made a wise move. He had me hold off on coaching and teaching *The Pack*, the mentality, and the offense. This was twofold. First, he realized what kind of season we were facing; and second, I had missed the fall season and the beginning of the spring with this team. He decided it was best to leave everything the same. It was the best decision that would pay huge dividends over the next two years. I learned so much from Coach Robe!

What he had me do instead was evaluate, help coach when I could, and recruit. Recruit I did. I was not with the team that much in 2012. I was, for the most part, on the road recruiting. That team would finish the season 23-30, miss the conference tournament, and hit .263 as a team with just 18 home runs.

The season culminated with a 17-0 loss in our last game of the year to the University of Louisiana-Monroe. Standing next to Coach Robe in the final innings of that game watching his misery and disgust, I looked at him and said, "Coach, don't worry. This will never happen again – 2013 is about to begin after this last out is made."

In the coming weeks we reshaped the roster, returning 15 players and bringing in 17 new recruits. The core was there. We just needed to mature and learn to play as a team. Ten players off that original team would go on to be vital members of one of the greatest teams in the history of UL just two years later.

Something encouraging happened at the end of April that year. Our home in College Station finally sold! Perfect timing! The season and the kids' school year was winding down and coming to an end. Sixteen months after going on the market, we were finally out from under that house at the exact right time. God is not always on our timetable, but He is never late. The hard part was looking for a place to live in Lafayette, which was another humbling experience. We had no money. We were looking for a home for a family of five, and the cost of living in Lafayette was a lot higher than it was in College Station. After an exhaustive search, we realized that we could not afford to live right inside Lafayette. That's when, once again, the Lord stepped in. While driving around one day in a little town south of Lafayette called Milton, we stumbled upon a 4-bedroom home in the middle of some sugar cane fields that had everything we needed. The home was for sale by owner, and they were willing to work with us. I was in no shape to get a loan, and that's when Coach Robe said, "Don't worry. Let me make a phone call." A week later, I had a loan and the money for the home. I love the Cajun culture! Only one more question to be answered: "How are we going to move?" We couldn't afford to pay movers, and we were moving five hours away, leaving a much larger home full of stuff. That's when Coach Robe said, "Don't worry" again and got a former player that owned a moving company to give us a great deal.

The move happened over a three-day span. We packed, loaded up, and set out for Lafayette. Reality had set in, once again, that I had created all of this; leaving Texas, moving out of state, coaching at a much smaller school for a much smaller salary, and to say we were "downsizing" would be an understatement. Kathy and the kids were nervous about the prospects of living in a new state, a new city, starting over with a new job, and starting new schools... yet again. "If only I had never drunk," is all I kept thinking.

When the movers pulled up to the house in Milton, things went from bad to worse. They couldn't fit all of our belongings in the house. Literally, half of our possessions were out on the driveway with nowhere to be stored. I said to Kathy, "Let's take a break, go eat, and come back." It was sunny when we left, but while at lunch a thunderstorm hit and it was raining all over our stuff on the driveway... so we thought. When we pulled back in, a few things had gotten wet, but the rest of it was covered by tarps. We have no clue, to this day, who did that for us. That sums up the Cajun culture.

When the movers came back in to finish, one of them casually dropped and broke something. That's when I snapped. I was at my breaking point, and I let all the movers have it. Kathy and Kyler were appalled. It only speaks to the condition of my heart then. Looking back, the condition of my heart actually matched that of the team I had just joined; both were broken. I would like to be able to say that I had quit drinking when I moved to Lafayette, but I hadn't. I was still running from the sins of my past, and many times I thought the best way to do that was to drown myself in alcohol. From March of 2012 through February of 2013, if I had to put a number on it, I would say I got drunk no less than 10-12 times. It was always by myself or in a very small setting so no one would know. I was still living a lie even after being blessed with a second chance and given so much grace. I can remember a phone call from one of my best friends, Dave Jorn, who was the pitching coach at the University of Arkansas at the time. "Jorny" was just calling to check in, and he asked at the end of our conversation, "How long you been sober now?" I hesitated and then said, "Oh, I don't know Jorny. I don't keep up with that sort of thing, but it's been a while." What a liar. If someone can't tell you how long they've been sober, they are lying!

Not even three days after moving the family to Lafayette, I got a call from another Division I school in Texas. They were offering me a job. Amazingly, 430 days outside of baseball and now I had a job and was being offered another one in the span of four months. I informed Coach Robe, and told him that Kathy and I were interested because it was back in Texas. Ever the gentleman, Coach Robe said he didn't want to lose us but he understood perfectly. Kathy and I drove back to Texas with the kids, took a look around, and came right back. I informed Coach Robe that I was seriously interested in the job. I even had the phone in my hand about to call and accept the position, but for some reason I didn't. Coach Robe asked if I would do him a favor and let him come over and meet with me, so on an early Saturday morning in June, we met privately for over four hours. That meeting helped save my life. I felt a connection to this man like never before. Something inside of me was saying, "This man will help save your life." After Coach Robe left, Kathy and I agreed right then and there to stay. I called and turned down the other job, then called my dad to tell him. He was ecstatic, as he had been telling me all along that we were going to do something amazing at UL, that I should be thankful to have that job, and to stay put. He's always been a visionary and has generally always been right.

Turns out, staying at UL was by far the best decision I could have ever made. However, it would still be a long, hard struggle to finally break free of all the chains that were binding me and escape the prison I was living in.

Pictured: Klaire, me, Kyler, and Khloe following a game at UL in the spring of 2012. Kathy and the kids had come over to visit one weekend, and this was the first time they had seen me back on the field and in uniform in a long time. The initial year was incredibly tough, but it was only setting the stage for two of the best years of my life. God really can take tragedy and turn it into triumph.

Story #22
Letting Go

"Forget the former things; do not dwell on the past. See, I am doing a new thing! Now it springs up; do you not perceive it? I am making a way in the wilderness and streams in the wasteland."
~ Isaiah 43:18-19

God had put this verse on my heart a year earlier when I was struggling to find a job, and He been giving me dreams and visions to show me what state I was in. Now I could not believe how good God was being to a sinner like me. I had already gotten an increase in my salary after being there a little less than a year and not doing much yet. Coach Robe had also given me total autonomy over the baseball side of the team. He even allowed me to hire Lance Harvell, a former player of mine that I was close to, who soon would become my right-hand man. However, I was still angry, bitter, and full of hate, not at any one person as much as at myself. I began to drink wine and other forms of alcohol around the house. Kathy was worn down by this time. She and the kids were exhausted and having a tough time settling in to the new surroundings. I was always careful to hide it from the kids as to not traumatize them, but the point is, I was drinking at home, once again...

I loved our team. I could tell we were going to be good. We were tough, loved to grind and work. I was working them as hard as I have ever worked a team. The only problem was, I was still living as a captive. I was still a prisoner of my own making and I was becoming increasingly more frustrated with the fact that the only thing that had changed was our zip code. There is no way this is what God intended. This was not

His plan when He poured His grace out upon me, but I just couldn't seem to break free from the lies, guilt, and shame that come with living a life of sin. The funny thing about guilt, shame, and feeling as if you're beyond repair is that it's unrelenting! It plays on loop in your mind 24/7, constantly reminding you that you're unworthy until you finally give in and believe every lie that your mind is telling you.

The five stages of grief are very real, and I had been reluctantly going through every one of them kicking and screaming for almost two years. Denial, anger, bargaining, depression, and acceptance are the five stages of grief. It seemed as if I went through them all at the same time, never truly passing from one stage to the next and always regressing back to a different stage. It was a vicious cycle that I thought would never end. I stayed in denial for years, at the same time carrying around white-hot anger, only to stop and try reasoning with myself over and over with the "what if's" and "if only's" of the bargaining phase. All the while, I was mired in the haze and fog of the depression that comes with such a loss. Then at times, for a brief instant, I would come to accept all that had come to pass. It was a matter of time before the entire process would start all over again. Then, one morning in the fall of 2012, God proved once again that you are never beyond His grasp, and that He does have the power to make ALL things new!

It was a Sunday like any other. My family and I were in church, a place we desperately needed to be. We were at Our Savior's Church, a non-denominational congregation in Lafayette, and had finally started to regularly attend, which was something we hadn't done in years, maybe never. I thought the church was just "OK," but Kathy and the kids had really grown to love it. I was grinding my way through the service, drifting my way in and out of self-hate, begging for forgiveness, and having an overall feeling of being "damaged goods." Thankfully, this Sunday was going to be different in a way that would begin to change my life, my family, and everyone around me. My youngest daughter, Khloe, who was just seven at the time, accepted the pastor's invitation to go up top to the baptismal tank and be baptized. This took me by total surprise, as my other two kids and wife sat in the pew. Khloe looked up at me and asked, "Daddy, will you go with me?" Embarrassed and still living a life of guilt and shame, I begrudgingly answered, "Sure, baby, I will take you." As we made our way up front, around the stage, and to the stairwell leading to the baptismal, we began to encounter what I thought was an unusually long line. As we waited in line and slowly began to make our way up the stairs, I remember something coming over me. Something was nudging my heart. It was an itch I just couldn't scratch. Finally, we reached the top, went into the bathroom, and changed into the shirt and robe they gave us.. We then reached the holding platform leading to the tank. We were third in line, and my heart was racing. Little Khloe was anxious as she was being led to hand her precious life over to Christ, and I was feeling unworthy. Not only unworthy as a man, but also unfit to be the one that escorted Khloe to her life-changing Baptism. I kept a good face and faked my way all the way to the pastor's outstretched arms. There he was, standing in the water and inviting Khloe to everlasting life. I was just along for the ride, the one Khloe innocently asked to escort her. As we entered the tank, the pastor asked, "Dad, do you want to take your daughter under, or do you want me to?" Immediately, without any hesitation, I decisively answered, "Nope! We are both going under today, brother." As hundreds of people in the congregation looked on, Khloe and I both went under that day.

Khloe was reaffirming a life that had already been saved, with the gift of Baptism. I, for the first time in years, was listening to God's voice. I did exactly what He spoke to me on the way into the water: "When you go under, give it all to me. Leave all the guilt, shame, anger and hate under the water." When we emerged, I suddenly felt lighter; not physically, but mentally and spiritually.

Although I instantly realized the impact of the commitment I had made, it would take several more years to realize the significance. That fateful Sunday morning, when Khloe, compelled by the urging of the Holy Spirit, decided to get baptized, triggered a powerful event. It would be the key to initially unlocking the chains of bondage I was living in. Bound by the constant lies of guilt and shame along with the inability to forgive myself, I was chained and living from the belief that I truly was damaged goods. If I had prayed once, then I had prayed a million times for the Lord to forgive the truly horrible things I had done. Never did I realize that God forgave me the first time I prayed that prayer. The only one that wasn't forgiving me, was me. I honestly believe that forgiving ourselves is the hardest thing to do and is the single biggest weapon that the enemy uses against us. By the Grace of God and through the power of the Holy Spirit, I finally forgave myself that morning. For the first time in years, I felt alive when I came up out of that water. I felt clean, light, and unburdened. I was determined not to carry anger, rage, resentment, and shame like a weight on my back any longer. Even though it sounds cliché, I *let go and let God* do His thing. Like a prisoner desperate for the key to the chains, I finally put both hands up and the Lord began to unlock them. Once again, the little girl that I had to sleep next to at night just to stay alive, a little over a year and a half earlier, had helped in saving my life.

Not long after the Baptism, I was still drinking. I wasn't drinking as much, nor to numb myself from the pain. Maybe it was out of habit or a lack of contentment, I don't know. One day I was sharing the Baptism with Coach Robe and we began talking. Coach Robe and I would often have long talks on life and such. Coach began to tell me what I would equate to a parable. He explained that if you have a spotless truck that you often wash and wax, when you are driving down the street and see a muddy pothole, what are you going to do? "The answer is simple," he said. "You are going to go around the pothole." Then he explained that if your truck is kind of clean and you see the same pothole, you will still go around. However, if you hit the edge of the pothole, it will be okay with you because your truck is not spotless. Then he made his point. If your truck is filthy and in need of washing, you not only will drive right through that muddy pothole; you will look for it! This simple story hit me right between the eyes and gave me a visual of the life I had been living. I needed to "clean my truck"! Coach Robe's wisdom, stories, and life experiences were like water in the middle of a desert. I soaked up every ounce of them. I can't tell you how many countless hours Coach Robe and I spent talking together after everyone had left from games or practices.

Later in the fall of 2012, Kyler and I enrolled in a mixed martial arts class together. The sensei was a Christian man that we simply knew as Sensei Micah. This man was a strong believer who was schooled at the black belt level in just about every martial art. He preached discipline with Christian values and was as tough a man as you will ever find. The discipline that I learned in Sensei Micah's dojo was something that began to stick with me, and slowly over the course of several months, I found that I was now living my life by those same tenets.

I was still drinking, but those days were starting to grow farther and farther apart. Now I was starting to feel remorse and sadness when I would drink. I felt like I was letting others down, not just myself. This was a new feeling for me, as I had always drunk to fulfill my own selfish desires.

The final unlocking of the chains of bondage happened early in the spring of 2013. This was an event that I didn't see coming, and it hit me right in the gut. In February, shortly after the season had begun, my best friend from childhood, Sean Matus, called to tell me his dad, JC, had died. JC had been very close to me growing up. He and my dad always coached Sean and me together in Little League. JC was like a second dad to me. Similar to my grandpa, JC was a man's man who worked hard his entire life at a refinery in Texas City. JC was tough, hard-working, and had a lot of charisma. He was the type of guy that people were always attracted to and liked to be around. Sean asked me if I could come to the funeral and deliver the eulogy. I told Sean I would be honored and that I would do whatever they needed. I remember we played LSU, and we got beat on a Tuesday, February 26. After the game I drove to Texas City for the funeral, which was set for the 27th. I would be missing one game against Nicholls State. At the time, I hadn't had a drink since New Year's Eve, almost two months. After the funeral we all went back to Sean's house. Someone suggested that we honor JC by drinking some Miller Lite, which was his favorite beer. While UL was playing Nicholls State, I was celebrating JC's life by drinking.

The next morning I got up at the crack of dawn, said my goodbyes, got in the truck, and headed back east to Lafayette. On the drive back, I was so mad at myself I couldn't see straight! I felt like I had let not only my family down again, but also my team and all of Lafayette. I was almost free. I could sense it, and the time was right for me to make a clean break and escape the chains I had lived in for so long. The following day it hit me like a ton of bricks. I always conducted what I call a *pack* meeting before, during, and after practice with the hitters (which I still do). While in our *pack* meeting following practice, still mad at myself, and disappointed in my actions the night before, I began to take a good slow look around at these kids, and what I saw had been right in front of me the entire time. We, including myself, were all broken. As I looked around, I saw that his dad was in prison, his mom has been married three times, his mom is an alcoholic, his dad is an alcoholic, his brother recently died, he's been suspended twice, and so on. We were all broken, and I was the chief broken one among us. I looked at those kids, and with tears in my eyes, I made a promise to myself that I will NEVER let them down and they will ALWAYS be able to depend and count on me. It was at that moment that I was finally free!!! I had proven over the years that I couldn't stop drinking for God, for my family, for myself, or my career; but God unlocked the final chain that day when I faced the brokenness in those boys' lives. I knew I would never drink again... for them. That's why I always say, when speaking of one of my teams, "I will always need them, way more than they need me."

I laid it all down on February 28, 2013, and haven't had a drink since. It's been almost five years. It wasn't easy. I had to clear some initial hurdles. After the season, at three months sober, I had a beer in my hand on a fishing trip; but I never opened it and put it down. At six months sober, on a hunting trip, the same thing. What I began to see was that the farther I got into my sobriety, the harder it was to surrender. My truck was finally clean, and I was determined not to drive through any potholes. Personally, I don't go to meetings. I'm not going to professional counseling, although I am not against either of these. For me, I give it all to God, stay connected to the Lord, take action, and do it for these boys. When I speak, I tell people, "You would have to put a gun to my head and pull the trigger before I would take another drink because if I drink again, I know I'm dead anyway."

Ultimately, all of the brokenness at UL would be the tie that would bind us and make us not only inseparable, but dang near unbeatable for the next two years!

Pictured: Khloe and me in the fall of 2012 at Our Savior's Church after getting baptized. That Baptism was the beginning of me "letting go." It's amazing how God uses and speaks through children. They truly are a gift from Him. After coming up out of the baptismal tank, I can't begin to explain how "free" I felt. It was the first time in years I felt like I wasn't in chains. I will never forget that feeling.

Pictured: Coach Robe and me before a game in 2014. There is no telling what we were talking about. We were constantly in conversation about so many things that were way more important than baseball. I learned so much from this man and will always owe him my life for helping to heal a family and a man that were totally broken. Coach Robe gave me a second chance when nobody else would.

Story #23
Defying the Odds

Pictured on previous page: "The Grinder" Jace Conrad following our regional championship win against Mississippi State in 2014 at Tigue Moore Field in Lafayette. We hosted that regional and lost the first game (1-0) against #4 seed Jackson State and then became one of only a handful of teams in college baseball history to come back and win their own regional after dropping their first game. We beat San Diego State, Jackson State, and Mississippi State twice to complete the comeback. These boys loved to compete, played hard, and were never ever out of the fight!

Now sober and living a life of total freedom, I was dangerous; and I mean that in a good way. I was now living in the truth and unafraid to share my journey with the team (or anyone else). The life I was now living, I was living as an open book and loving it. I was starting to become the man, husband, dad, friend and coach that God had made me to be. There is an absolute fearlessness that comes from living a life of faith, taking action, and doing something about it. For me, Faith + Action = ALL THINGS ARE POSSIBLE. I was not only living this now, I was seeing the fruits of it through my family, our individual players, and our team with each passing day. The more I sacrificed, the more God continued to shine down upon me, my family, and this team.

Kathy and the kids were not only adjusted to Lafayette, they were loving it! To this day, we still all consider Lafayette our second home. The kids were excelling in school and Kathy was the Mother's Day Out coordinator at our church and doing a great job. They loved her. We had all gone from just surviving to now thriving!

At the same time, our players were crushing it in the mid to later parts of the 2013 season. It had taken a while, but they now had a full grasp of *The Pack Mentality* and were eating it up. Loving every second of it, the team (as a whole) was doing just as well. We had now entered the national conversation and had put together a resume worthy of the postseason. We had done all of this with our potent *Pack* offense. These guys could bang! When I say bang, I mean they could really hit, and hit is what they did. We had gone from a team that hit just .263 with only 18 home runs the year before to a *Pack* that was leading the nation in just about every offensive category. Coach Robe had always preached, "You have to *give* up to *go* up." That's exactly what we were all doing, players and coaches included. We were all dialed in, focused, and willing to sacrifice. We were willing to do whatever it took for each other. We were beginning to see the fruits of our hard work and sacrifice. The wave of momentum was now rolling. Gone was the team and the coach that were broken. Our mantra was, "Every man needs a second chance every now and then." We played and coached with that type of freedom and fearlessness.

The city of Lafayette and the surrounding areas of south Louisiana (Acadiana) had embraced us, and we had embraced them. Theirs is a culture unlike anything we had ever seen, where family comes first. Hard work, fight, and the love and passion to compete are valued above all else. Cajuns are helpers and doers. They are always eager to serve and live life with a joy that is seemingly unmatched. They are never in a hurry and never stress over the small things. Like I said, it's all about family and love. We grew and learned so much during our time there. We are only where we are now, as a family, because of our time with our "Cajun" family. We absolutely love the Cajuns. It's ironic, and I mentioned it earlier, that God would take someone with a drinking problem and put him and his family in the middle of a place that loves so much to have a good time with family, friends, and adult beverages. He used this place to help me get sober. Unbelievable, but that's the way it happened.

The 2013 team would go on to finish with a bang. We had gone from a 23-30 record the year before, not even qualifying for the conference tournament, to now playing for the regular season conference title. We missed winning the conference by one game. Then we hosted and advanced to the championship game of the conference tournament only to get beat by Florida Atlantic, who had the best pitcher in the league. By that time, our resume was outstanding, and on "Selection Monday" we heard our name called as the #2 seed in the Baton Rouge regional. Strangely enough, the #3 seed in that regional was none other than Sam Houston State University. We would ultimately advance all the way to the championship game against host school, LSU. We lost 5-1, but the stage was set for what would become one of the most unbelievable seasons by any team in college baseball history. The 2013 team had just defied the odds and completed the largest turnaround in the NCAA, going from 23-30 in 2012 to 43-20 the very next year. In addition to that, the team that had hit just .263 with 18 home runs the year before, had now become the #1 ranked offense in the country. More than 300 teams in the country play Division I baseball, and the *Pack* was the #1 offense. Wow! In 2013, we led the nation in home runs with 72 and slugging percentage at .513. We were 2nd in the nation in batting average (.323) and total bases (1057). We were 3rd in hits with 666, ranked 4th in runs scored (453), doubles (137), and were 6th in runs per game (7.7). The 2013 team ranked in the top 10 nationally in eight different categories. In conference play, the Cajuns offense was ranked #1 in 10 different categories. By the time 2014 rolled around, we were a well-oiled machine. We returned over 20 players and we were as confident as ever with big expectations. I will never forget in a *Pack* meeting early that fall, we were talking about our vision. We all knew that we were chasing Omaha and the College World Series, but the first part of our vision is always a benchmark of wins. I said, "40 plus," and several of the players shot back immediately with, "Nah, Coach, we are winning 50 plus!" I said, "Okay, 50 plus. Let's do it." Then I thought to myself, "These guys are crazy! No way."

We began the season ranked something like 15th nationally, and nobody was happy with it. We felt slighted, and the chip on our shoulder was only growing bigger and bigger. We opened up against Eastern Illinois. With expectations through the roof, we laid an egg and lost 5-1. We then reeled off 10 straight wins. The last six consecutive wins came by sweeping Southern Mississippi on the road three games, beating LSU on the road, and taking two of three vs. Alabama at home.

The first game, of what was an important series vs. Alabama, was a memorable one. It was on February 28, the one-year anniversary of my sobriety, a feat I once thought was impossible. We were in a pitcher's duel with their #1 pitcher vs. our #1 pitcher. In the last inning of a 0-0 game, we executed a perfect "double squeeze" play to seal the win. That night was very special for me, as the stadium was packed and rowdy, and it was a big win for us, at the time. I could feel God shining His grace down upon me that night, as if to say, "I'm proud of you."

We lost the finale of the Alabama series that Sunday, and then we reeled off 14 in a row after that. By this time, everyone knew that something special was happening in Lafayette. We were ranked as a team in the top 10 in the country at that point, and we were leading the country in offense again. Towards the end of the season, at one point, we were ranked #1 in 27 out of 30 offensive categories; and now we had the pitching to match it. We were a scary team to play. Our players were physical, played as a team, had a huge chip on their shoulders, and did everything with bad intentions. We played fast, hard, loose, and we had fun. We were good and we knew it. However, there was also a humility and sacrificial side to it. This entire run had been founded on Biblical, eternal principles. The underlying mantra all along (as I mentioned before) was, "Every man needs a second chance every once in a while." This was displayed by the fact that on Thursdays or Fridays before home games, we would let the prisoners from the parish jail, in orange jumpsuits and all, come on the field and take batting practice with us. The boys loved it, and we quickly became the most popular people within the parish jail. This act of kindness spoke to the heart of the team. It spoke to where we had all come from, what we had overcome, and where we were now. We had no rules. We were all living in total freedom, and it was the time of my life. Instead of practicing, we would watch a movie in the clubhouse. Coach Robe would have the concessions people come in with popcorn and Coke for everyone. It was awesome! We watched "Lone Survivor" no less than four times that year. Instead of Thursday night practice, we would go watch a minor league or big league game, depending on what city we were in. Coach Robe always had Bible study available on Wednesdays and chapel on Sundays. We were winning, but we were doing it "our" way. We were winning at the things we controlled. One time, before a Friday night game in Arlington, we spent the entire day touring AT&T Stadium, home of the Cowboys; that culminated in an all-out football game down on the field. It happened to be Easter weekend, so on Sunday we skipped batting practice so everyone could go to church. The day before the conference tournament championship game in Mobile, Alabama, instead of practicing, we took the entire team to the beach all day. With sunburns and all, we beat the University of Texas at Arlington 6-5 on a 7th-inning home run by Blake Trahan, to win the Sunbelt Conference tournament.

We finished the 2014 regular season, including the conference tournament, by winning 10 in a row. We captured the regular season conference championship and broke a school record with 26 wins and four losses. We won the conference tournament and went on to become the first "mid-major" school in college baseball history to finish the regular season as the consensus #1 ranked team in the country in all five polls. This cast of "nobodies" who set out collectively, with broken hearts and all, to become "somebody" had now shocked the baseball world, defied the odds, and pulled off the impossible. We then topped the regular season by becoming the first team in school history to be a top eight national seed. As a result, we were selected to host a regional and super regional. ESPN came to Lafayette and captured the entire event during their "Selection Monday" show. We hosted the show at the stadium. The stands were packed; all our families, the team, and the rest of the community were there. It was simply amazing! To think of where we had come from (personally and as a team), in less than two years, was nothing short of miraculous.

Our regional consisted of Jackson State, San Diego State, and Mississippi State, who was fresh off an appearance in the national title game a year earlier. We opened up the regional the exact same way we started the season, by losing 1-0 to #4 seed, Jackson State. Everyone was in full panic mode, embarrassed and thinking we were now done. On my drive home that night, I remember telling myself to suck it up, put on a good face, and be nice to everyone when I got to the house. (We had some of our family staying with us that weekend.) To my surprise, shortly after walking in, Kathy, who in the past because of my actions generally didn't get caught up in wins or losses, said something short and rude to me. Since I was trying to be nice, I said, "What's wrong with you, babe?" I thought I had done something wrong. She proceeded to say, "I can't believe y'all lost! Y'all have now made it so hard to win this regional, I'm not ready for this to be over." I had to chuckle to myself because I realized she had become invested, and this was just further proof on how far we had truly come as a family.

The next day I was as confident as ever, not only in us as a team, but also in who I was becoming as a man. I gathered the hitters early for a *Pack* meeting and informed them that we were going to come back and win this regional by winning four straight, and this was how I knew. Then I read them one of my favorite Bible passages, 1 Corinthians 1:26-31:

Brothers and sisters, think of what you were when you were called. Not many of you were wise by human standards; not many were influential; not many were of noble birth. But God chose the foolish things of the world to shame the wise; God chose the weak things of the world to shame the strong. God chose the lowly things of this world and the despised things—and the things that are not —to nullify the things that are, so that no one may boast before him. It is because of Him that you are in Christ Jesus, who has become for us wisdom from God—that is, our righteousness, holiness and redemption. Therefore, as it is written: "Let the one who boasts boast in the Lord."

I read these verses because they matched up perfectly with who we were – a bunch of misfits that shared a common bond of love, unity, and a passion to compete. We beat San Diego

State 9-2. The following day we beat Jackson State 11-1 and Mississippi State 14-8, to set up a Monday "winner take all" championship game. We won that game 5-3. Comeback complete! We were now regional champions. The following week we hosted a talented Ole Miss team in the super regional. We won the first game 9-5, to complete the most dominating five-game stretch I have ever been blessed to be a part of. To their credit, Ole Miss came back and beat us in two close games over the next couple of days, thus ending our dream of getting to Omaha.

Even though we didn't get to Omaha, that didn't diminish what had been done. The 2014 Ragin' Cajuns led the nation in offense once again, ranking either #1 or #2 in the country in nine different offensive categories. That team went wire to wire in the top 25 national rankings. They finished at #7 in the country, never lost back-to-back games until the last two of the year, and finished 58-10, which was only two wins away from the all-time record. They said before they started that they were going to win 50 plus, and I will be danged if they didn't do it. Eleven players off the 2013-2014 teams went on to play professionally.

Those two and half years were so much more than just baseball, setting records, and national rankings. They were about relationships, redemption, love, healing, and learning to live a life of sacrifice. They were about family, simplicity, standing up, taking action, and making the most of a second chance. Most of all, those two and a half years will always stand as living proof that yes, God does use broken things. He takes those that have scars and uses them to defy the odds, and that's exactly what we did.

CAJUNS BEAT THE ODDS

UL players and coaches celebrate following their 5-3 victory over Mississippi State in an NCAA Regional baseball game at M.L. "Tigue" Moore Field. PAUL KIEU, THE ADVERTISER

Pictured: Me in the center and Coach Robe right behind me. This photo and caption, crazy enough, came out on the front page of the local paper after we beat Mississippi State to win the 2014 regional. That picture really tells the entire story. "He has made everything beautiful in its time. He has also set eternity in the human heart; yet no one can fathom what God has done from beginning to end."

~ Ecclesiastes 3:11

Pictured: The Pack and me giving thanks to the Lord for blessing us to all be together at that moment in time. Yes, we had just won a championship, but we were all fortunate just to be there. There were so many stories of redemption on that team. God truly had taken tragedy and turned it into triumph.

Pictured: The 2014 Cajun Pack, the last photo we ever took together after losing to Ole Miss. Many of them were leaving to go play professionally. Kathy, the kids, and I would soon be packing up and heading to Huntsville, Texas. If you look closely, they are all holding a book in their hands. It's a daily devotional that Kathy bought for each one of them. How far we had come!

Story #24
Going Home

Grace is so incredible that it doesn't take you back to the beginning; it takes you to the place you would have been if you had been faithful the entire time. That is how grace works in relation to destiny.

~ Luke Holter, *Filthy Fishermen*

...What he opens no one can shut, and what he shuts no one can open. I know your deeds. See, I have placed before

you an open door that no one can shut. I know that you have
little strength, yet you have kept my word and have not
denied my name.
~ Revelation 3:7-8

In a strange way, my being fired was turning into an incredible blessing. I never could have fathomed it at the time. Had I not been fired and unable to find a job, had so many doors not been closed, I wouldn't be where I was, doing what I was doing. My life was on the wrong path, and the destiny I was trying to fulfill was only leading me down the road to my own destruction. There is no doubt in my mind that God orchestrated every single aspect of what was happening, down to the tiniest detail. The story God was weaving together in my life would not be possible by mere man. No one could orchestrate these events. Too many specific things had to take place to put me where I was, at the exact time I was there.

Doors were being opened, and opportunity was coming my way. There were at least two opportunities to go back to the SEC as an assistant and an offer to head back to the Big XII, but none of that now interested me. I had gone back to my roots. I'm an underdog and always have been. I'm a David vs. Goliath kind of guy. Maybe it's just who I am, I don't know; but I had been there and done that. I was learning how to live a life of contentment. Life in the fast lane just wasn't for me anymore, and I was very much enjoying the simple life. The only way I was leaving Coach Robe and UL was to be a head coach. I knew that being a head coach had always been my calling, but I was growing frustrated with that as well. Over the course of the previous year and a half, I had interviewed for three head coaching jobs, two in the Southland Conference and one in Conference USA. I didn't come close to getting any of them. In fact, two of the three interviews were on the phone. Therefore, when the Sam Houston State University head coaching job came open at the end of our 2014 season, I just pushed it to the back of my mind and carried on with business as usual for well over a week. I just wasn't in the frame of mind to jump through hoops, only to be disappointed again. In my mind, I knew UL wanted me and everyone else, I thought, perceived me as damaged goods. Besides that, we were just coming off a crushing defeat in the super regional, and I knew we had an "Omaha" type team coming back in 2015. I didn't want to go through the rejection all over again. *(On a side note, the 2015 UL team made it all the way back to a super regional, narrowly losing to LSU to get to Omaha.)*

Late one June afternoon, after we finished our last exit meeting with the 2014 team, I headed home to finally take a deep breath and unwind. As Kathy and I were talking later that evening, I said, "Hey, you know the SHSU job is open?" Her immediate reaction was, "Well, you are definitely going to apply for that job, aren't you?" I said, "No, I'm done applying for jobs." Instantly, she sat up and said, "No, you're not. You're going to apply for that job." After thinking about it for a minute, I said: "Well, I do still have Bobby Williams' cell number from when I phone interviewed a few years ago. I will send him a text. If it's meant to be, that will be enough to open the door. That's all I'm doing, though." It was 10:30pm, and Kathy shot back with, "Well, then text him!" At 10:30 at night, I simply sent Bobby Williams, the AD at SHSU, a text.

The prompting of Kathy and the simple action of sending Bobby a text was enough to open a crack in the door, and God took over from there. I did ultimately apply and go through a rigorous interviewing process, but it was all worth it. On June 28, 2014, Kathy and I not only celebrated our 17th wedding anniversary – we were also celebrating the fact that we were "going home," as SHSU had called to offer me the job!

The following week, I left for Huntsville as Kathy and the kids stayed behind to sell the house and take care of all the loose ends. The same day the *For Sale* sign was put in the front yard, the house sold for $10,000 more than we were asking! Yes, that's right. The home sold in one day. That's 15 months and 30 days faster than it took to sell our house in College Station. It's amazing how God works in your life when you are living in His Will!

At the same time, Coach Robe was finalizing a deal to hire JT as my replacement – the same man who had been through so much yet so unselfishly helped me get a job in pharmaceuticals. He helped me get in the door with the Cajuns and was now going to be back in baseball after five years out of the game. God is good!

It was a seller's market when we were looking for homes to buy, and we were having trouble deciding on where the kids were going to go to school until a lifelong friend of mine sent me a text one day. He went to school at SHSU and wanted to congratulate me on the job. At the end of the text, he stated that Huntsville has an incredible private Christian school. One afternoon we drove out Highway 30 to look at the school. As we were turning in, I noticed a neighborhood across the street. Instead of making a left to the school, I made a right into the neighborhood. They only had two houses for sale. With one simple drive out Highway 30, we found a school and a house. Our kids go to school right across the street from where we live. Thank you, Jesus!

It didn't take long after arriving at SHSU to realize that we had struck gold. What an incredible university! The Bearkats had been successful over the last seven or eight years, prior to our arrival. The coaches and teams before us had already laid the groundwork and tradition that made a strong foundation for us to build on. The first thing I realized was that SHSU has the three things that it takes, in my mind, to win and sustain that winning on a national stage. I really believed we had the opportunity to take SHSU to new heights. We have invaluable support from a president and AD that have great vision and love to win. We also have an incredibly loyal fan base and community, as well as alumni and a donor base that loves to help. We have some of the best baseball facilities for any "mid-major" in the country that continue to improve, thanks to our very generous donors. We have, what I think, is the best location of any school in the state. Huntsville is a beautiful city that is located just an hour north of Houston, on the I-45 corridor. It's not too close but not too far, either. It's just right.

We understood and realized, from the get-go, that this place (SHSU) was ready to explode. With these three factors in place, we hit the ground running. We rolled up our sleeves and worked harder than ever, establishing the same culture of love and overachievement that we had brought to life in Lafayette. We knew it wouldn't happen overnight, but we also knew it was entirely possible to build a program on the bedrock of *Faith, Sacrifice, Obedience, and Service*. From there, we set off to take this program to places it had never been and to heights that no one thought possible. In three short years, that's exactly what we have done.

The school, community, and region have rallied around our program and these players with unending loyalty and support. These boys are lovable. Their style of play and love for each other are contagious. Win or lose, they are hard not to like. They are blue-collar, hard-nosed, loyal, and work harder than any group I have ever had. I love these boys like they are my own. Just like the players at UL, they keep me going. Next to my own family, they are my family. That's all our program is really, one big family. I think people are attracted to that. We are old-fashioned and "old school" in our approach to the way we do things. We help, we serve, we show up early, and we work. We don't want anything given to us, and we don't make excuses. We will earn whatever we get; and all our coaches, players, and their families understand that.

Over the last three years, on the field, we have been able to take this program to the next level. We have been able to break records and make history. All of that is great and something that makes my heart smile, but it is not what my identity is tied to. What really brings me joy is the fact that eight players have accepted Christ as their Lord and Savior over the last seven months. Spending every Wednesday night in Bible study with our players and sharing my story with these young men is what fills my cup. Our relationships in the community, our service off the field, and the fact that we have a team GPA of 3.3 are the areas where we are really winning big. That's what means the most to me. Wins, losses, and stats are all temporary and fleeting. I want to be judged by the men we are helping to develop and the life-long relationships that we are making.

I often get asked, "When are you going to leave? We know you are going to take a bigger job." My response is the same every time: "We aren't going anywhere. We are home. Lafayette is our adopted home, Texas City is our birth home, and Huntsville is the place we call home." We love it here! I don't ever want to be where I cannot have impact. Sam Houston, the administration, and the community allow me, through my story, to have impact. Not only do they allow it, they applaud it. That is very rare and something I don't take for granted. Sam Houston State and the community gave me a second chance at being a head coach when no one else would.

They love us and we love them. Their loyalty, commitment, and willingness to help rival that of which we witnessed with the Ragin' Cajuns. That is what it takes at a school of this size. It takes all of us. This community and university embrace that. We are ever so thankful to be right here, right now, surrounded by such love and support.

My true destiny in Christ is now being fulfilled by trusting God and living a life of *Faith + Action*. I have found my true calling. I have realized the difference between fate and destiny. Fate is when you don't take action. Destiny is when you wake up each day and do something about it by taking action. I choose to do something about it. I choose to fulfill God's destiny for my life. Once broken and a prisoner to a life of sin, I am now whole and living a life of total freedom. My mission is no longer Omaha, big jobs, money, notoriety, recognition, or chasing the temporary things of this world. My "new mission" is to build well-rounded men and teach them that their identity is not tied to what they do, but to who they are in Christ by "transforming," not "transacting." My "new mission" is to help change lives, and do so by sharing God's amazing story that He has placed on my life.

Coach Robe handed me a sheet of paper one day, towards the end of the 2013 season. It listed the stages of the life of a successful, well-rounded man. I still have it. It said, "Your 20's are for learning, your 30's are for editing, your 40's are for mastering, your 50's are for harvesting, and your 60's are for guiding." If this is true, which I believe it is, I have taken what I have learned, edited the mistakes, and now have begun to master who I am, not in baseball, but in Christ.

I can't wait for the harvest...

Pictured: Pastor Nick Carroll and his wife, Rachel, of Our Savior's Church in Lafayette; along with me, Khloe, Kathy, Kyler, and Klaire in the summer of 2014. They brought us on stage to honor us and pray for us before we left for Huntsville. It's amazing to think how far God had brought us in just two years... from a family and a man that were broken, to Khloe and me being baptized, to now being honored on stage... truly amazing.

Pictured: Kyler, Khloe, and Klaire at our house in Lafayette the day it was put up for sale. Unlike our house in College Station that took 16 months to sell after I was fired, our home in Lafayette sold on the first day, shortly after this picture was taken. It's amazing what happens when you walk and live in the Will of God.

Pictured: Jay Sirianni, me, and Lance Harvell following our historic regional championship at the Lubbock regional in June of 2017. Just three years after "going home." Sam Houston State University has been all that I imagined and then some. We are truly blessed to get to be a part of this.

Pictured: Coaches Jay Sirianni, Lance Harvell, and Shane Wedd before a game in the dugout. Having fun is so much a part of what we do. Not much of anything is out of bounds and everyone is fair game. We work together, we coach together, we hunt together, we work out, and even play pick-up basketball together. We pretty much do life together. When you are with the guys you work with, as much or more than your own family, you better make sure there is a tight-knit bond. These dudes are not only pros, they are family and some of my best friends in the world. There is no greater honor than to get to do what I do and get to do it alongside these men.

Chapter 7
God's Promises Are Real

"Unless you people see signs and wonders," Jesus told him, "you will never believe."
~ John 4:48

Along this incredible journey there were several times that God smiled down at me and winked… as if to say, "Keep going, don't quit. Just keep going, I got you." This chapter is an account of some of the signs, wonders, and promises that God placed in my life at a time when I needed them most. I couldn't make any of this up. My imagination is not that good. God's timing and will are always perfect and beyond belief.

Story #25
From The Walls to The Ark

One of the many interesting things about Huntsville, Texas, is that it is home to the state prison system, and the main unit is called The Walls unit. This unit is where the prisoners are released. It is also where some of them are put to death. The Walls unit is located about three blocks behind our left field wall. One block down from our right field wall, at the bottom of a hill, is a cemetery. The cemetery is also part of the prison system. It's for all the men who die in prison but are never claimed by loved ones, or do not have the money for a proper burial. Consequently, they are all buried (unclaimed) in the same cemetery. I live approximately seven miles from the stadium and three miles outside the Huntsville city limits as you head down Highway 30 West, towards College Station.

There is a multitude of ways that I could drive to my office at the stadium every day, and I have pretty much tried them all. The route I like most isn't the fastest or the easiest. There are three or four more desirable ways to get there, but this route means the most to me. Therefore, it's the one that I choose to take to work almost every day. The route goes like this: I pull out of my neighborhood and turn left on Highway 30 East. I drive about five miles into town until Highway 30 turns into 11th Street. Then I stay on 11th until I get to Avenue I. Next, I hang a right. The reason I go right at Avenue I is because right there in front of me is The Walls unit. It's a huge intimidating structure with four giant, reddish-brown walls. There are guard towers high atop each corner and one in the middle. At first glance, this Walls unit is dark, daunting, and very scary looking. However, it is none of that to me. I look at that prison every day, and I praise and thank the Lord because, be it not for the grace of God, I should be in there! Then I take a deep breath and remind myself that the only thing more agonizing than living in an actual prison where someone put you is living in a prison of your own making where you put yourself! There are people in that prison that are living more freely than I ever was as a captive in my own web of lies and deceit. Then I promise myself that I will NEVER go back to being a captive again, and that I am less than the least of any person in that prison. I was given a second chance, a new lease; I was redeemed, and I WILL make the most of it.

That's why I drive by that prison every day, but that's just the beginning of my daily journey to get to Don Sanders Stadium, located on the eastern edge of campus at Sam Houston State University. Just south of the prison, and the next thing I pass every morning, is the Huntsville Feed Mill and Store. That's right – behind the prison is a feed store and small mill. I can't make this stuff up, but it gets better. After I pass the feed mill, I cross over 15th Street, only then to reach campus. As I turn left to head to the stadium, I pass our church, "The Ark," which is located on campus in the Lowman Student Center. Let me recap this for you. I am privileged to get up each day and drive to a job I love and have so much passion for; the route actually passes by a prison, a feed mill, then crosses over 15th Street, gets to campus, then passes our church before turning into the stadium.

Consider this: (1) I was living in a prison of my own making and lost everything, (2) only to wind up unemployable and working at a feed mill. (3) Fifteen had been my only number my entire coaching career until I got fired. (4) The university I was restored back to (5) only after I turned my life around through God and the church.

I challenge you to find another university in the country that can map a route in accordance to the redemption God has poured out on me in chronological order. I believe this is a daily reminder of God's grace in my life.

When I go home at night, I go a completely different route. On some days, the route takes me east on Bowers Boulevard down the right field side of our stadium, down the hill to a stop sign. When I look to my right, I see the cemetery of the unclaimed prisoners and say a prayer. I actually say a verse for all of these men. It comes from Ecclesiastes 3:11: *"God makes all things beautiful in His time, and he plants eternity in the hearts of all men; no one can fathom what God has done from beginning to end."* Then I remind myself that the world might not have wanted these men, but you know what? If their hearts were right, their eternal Father does. No one wanted me but one man, Tony Robichaux. That one man didn't care about my past, and wiped the slate clean. Never, ever, ever underestimate the power of a second chance.

Pictured: The Walls Unit is the very first thing I see as I turn right onto Avenue I every morning on my way to Don Sanders Stadium.

Pictured: Just south of The Walls Unit and right behind the prison, is Huntsville Farm Supply, a small feed store and mill...

Pictured: The first building I pass after the feed mill as I enter the campus at Sam Houston State University...

Pictured: Just before I turn left to head to the Stadium after I enter campus is the Lowman Student Center... home to The Ark on Sundays... the church that we call home.

Pictured: "15ᵗʰ Street" sign – Looking back, separates the university and our church from the feed mill and prison, which serves as a stark reminder of how quickly things can go wrong if you are not on guard and feeding yourself mentally, physically, and spiritually on a daily basis.

Pictured: The speed limit on the street I turn down to head to the stadium. Crazy that the speed limit is 15 (my former number), and the message is to remind you that the street will flood. Our house was totally flooded, if you recall, prior to my entering rehab... yet again, another reminder.

Pictured: The beautiful entrance towards Don Sanders Stadium on the corner of Sycamore and Bowers is the last thing I see before entering our parking lot each morning. You can see our scoreboard in the background. We are so very blessed!

Story #26

Lonely Palm

In chapter five, I wrote about the visions that were occurring in the summer of 2011, and I wrote of one vision specifically. The vision was of four vibrant, healthy, beautiful palms; and at the end of the row, there was one lonely palm. This palm was brown, withered, and looked like it had gone through a storm the strength of a hurricane. It was bare, leaning over to one side, and it looked as if it were going to be dead soon. All five of these palms were for sale at what looked like some sort of huge marketplace. The entire place was packed, and one person after another was coming up to look at these beautiful palms and the gorgeous planters that were holding them. That's when God spoke into my heart that everyone would buy the beautiful palms, but the ugly, withered palm represented me in my current condition and that no one was going to buy me. He promised, however, that someday they would. After that, God led me to verses in the Bible that I had never come across before. The verses came out of the book of Job:

> *But if you will seek God earnestly*
> *and plead with the Almighty,*
> *if you are pure and upright,*
> *even now he will rouse himself on your behalf*
> *and restore you to your prosperous state.*
> *Your beginnings will seem humble,*
> *so prosperous will your future be.*
> ~ *Job 8: 5-7*

What I didn't tell you in chapter 5 was the rest of the story. Here is the rest of the story all the way to present day... That Bible passage really stuck with me throughout the summer of

2011 and gave me a glimmer of hope in the midst of everything I was going through. I was, at the time, unemployed and no one in college baseball would touch me. Then, after the summer heading into the fall of 2011, I really didn't think about those verses much again. I didn't land a job in baseball, went to work in the feed mill, and then went on to sell pharmaceuticals. It wasn't until I landed back on my feet at UL in March of 2012 that the verses really began to dawn on me again. When I left A&M, I was making big money. Kathy didn't have to work, our kids were in private school, and we didn't want for anything, although we were still living beyond our means. When I was hired at UL, I began at a salary that was approximately 1/4 of my old salary, give or take. That's when I thought about the vision and the verse again for the first time in months.

Your beginnings will seem humble, so prosperous your future will be. Faith in that verse began to motivate me, knowing that God had something big in store. Not five months later, my salary was doubled when I was considering an offer from a school in Texas. I ultimately decided to stay in Lafayette and, thank God, we did; but nonetheless we were now making double the original salary. Then we had the huge turnaround in 2013, and again I was handsomely rewarded. At the culmination of the historic run we made in 2014, my salary had now come full circle to almost matching the base salary I was making at A&M. God truly is amazing.

After three years at Sam Houston State, God has continued to shine His light brightly upon us. His Word and the vision He put in my heart continue to come true year after year. After our record-breaking season in 2017, I signed a five-year contract that was also record-breaking, not only for this university, but for the Southland Conference as well. Pretty amazing if you think about the fact that just six years earlier we had blown through our savings and our retirement, and maxed out every credit card to make ends meet. To go from your kids being on a free and reduced lunch plan to signing a record-breaking deal just six years later is nothing short of a God thing! My "beginnings" were indeed very humble, but I can promise you this: Since the day I decided to put the alcohol down and live a life motivated by Faith, Sacrifice, Obedience, and Service to the Lord... our "future" has been nothing but fruitful and prosperous. God's Word and promises are very much alive and real.

While the financial rewards and gains are nice, the Lord is doing something so much bigger here. Another way of looking at this verse and the Promise God made to me through a vision is this: Yes, God restored us back to financial prosperity and yes, he has taken us to new heights financially, but that is only half of the vision. The way I see it is that God took a transactional coach and over time humbled him and transformed him. Now the transactional coach is a transformational coach that is serving to help motivate, inspire and change lives. God has opened so many more doors, placed me on much bigger stages... and used His story through me to help transform lives. *Your beginnings will seem humble, so prosperous will be your future...* It's not so much about the temporary rewards, although they are a blessing, as much as the eternal promises of God's Word. I am thankful for both. And I am still amazed that... *I was once a palm that was dying and now people see me as worthy of buying.*

Pictured: Me addressing a huge crowd that had gathered to send us off to the super regional in Tallahassee, Florida, in June of 2017. Our beginnings were very humble, just as the Lord promised: From a feed mill, to selling pharmaceuticals, to starting over at UL, and then to Sam Houston State. But... God is faithful and His Word is the absolute truth. Prosperous and fruitful has been our future... just like He said it would be.

Story #27

The Ticket Stub

One of the hardest parts of being fired was waking up each morning with nowhere to go. I was used to waking up to a routine, and every minute of the early part of the day generally mattered. Not so when you are unemployed. I would wake up, the kids would leave for school, and my wife left for her job. Everyone had somewhere to go but me. This was an agonizing experience and a very lonely existence. So much of what we did at A&M was relational. I was missing that side of things immensely. It would not be uncommon for us to sit around and shoot the bull in one of our offices for an hour or so, three to four times a week. Now it was just me, at the house, all alone, left to ponder where it all went wrong and what I was going to do next. Even though I was a mess and still drinking, I could no longer stand the feeling of not having anywhere to go.

After a couple of months, I decided to try to beat my feelings of loneliness by working out again. Not having a gym to go to, I would improvise by doing push-ups, swimming laps, and jogging. I began to establish a good routine by getting up early before the kids and Kathy left, then eating and working around the house. Around mid-morning, I would do push-ups and go on a three-mile run around the trail in our neighborhood. I even got to the point where I was timing myself, which was pretty good considering the shape I was in both mentally and physically at the time. After the run, I would come back and swim laps for 30 minutes or so. After the workout, I would eat lunch. Around mid-afternoon, I would figure out a way to drink until Kathy and the kids got home. I had a routine going, but at the same time I was a mess, a liar, and a drunk. I was still miserable and feeling hopeless, like there was no end in sight. Waking up, no matter what kind of routine I was in, was still agonizing. The only relief I felt was usually just before going to sleep each night. I really did not know how I was going to make it through from one day to the next.

Then, something very strange happened. It was one of those things that you just can't explain. It just happened. I had done my push-ups and had started out on my daily jog. About a mile into it, I happened to spot something out of the corner of my eye. It was lying there in the grass, just off the sidewalk. I normally would not have stopped because once I started running, I never stopped – I needed all the momentum I could get to make it all the way around the three-mile track. This day was different. Something in my gut told me to stop and see what was laying there. After jogging about 30 yards past it, I stopped, turned around, and walked back to see what it was. To my surprise, it was an unused ticket to a Sam Houston State Bearkat Baseball game. I picked it up, put it in my pocket, put a smile on my face, and continued with my jog.

Remember, the year was 2011. I had no affiliation with Sam Houston State and I was living in College Station, but I could feel God nudging my heart as I continued to run. I truly believe the Lord was speaking truth into my life and urging me to "press on" by giving me a glimpse into the future. It was as if He were saying, "Keep going, don't quit. There are big things in store." When I found out the Sam Houston State head baseball coaching position was open in the early part of the summer of 2014, my mind went directly back to that jog, three years earlier.

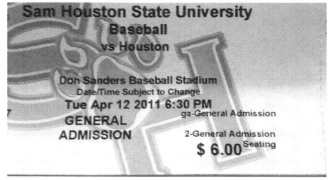

Pictured: a Bearkat baseball ticket from the spring of 2011

*Things like this have continued to happen to me
throughout this journey and have served to keep me going
even when I was at some of my lowest points. God has
continued, no matter how low I was, to wink at me, hold me
by the hand, and urge me to keep going.*

Story #28

28:15

I mentioned earlier that 15 had been my number during
my entire career. I had not only submersed my identity in
baseball for years, I had also tied my identity to the number
15. No matter what team I was a part of, nobody was going to
wear #15 except for me. That's who I was. I was living a front,
with my identity in baseball, all the while hiding behind a
number. That number, I thought, gave me strength, made me
who I was, and in some weird way completed me. By now,
after reading most of my story, you can see how well that was
working for me. When I threw it all away for alcohol and a
life of sin, the front was exposed and there was no longer a
number to hide behind. I was all alone for everyone to see
who I really was. The rest of the story behind the number 15 is
that when I got to UL in early March of 2012, the season was
already under way and they only had one number left. In fact,
they didn't even have a pair of turf shoes in my size. I had to
go buy my own. I love it now, looking back. Remember the
verse out of Job? *So, humble your beginnings will be...* Over
the course of the last 430 days, I had been totally humbled,
and now was no different. Before our first game, the manager
took me to the equipment room to get a uniform, and guess
what? There was no #15. That number was already being
worn. In fact, there was only one number left – #28. The

198

interesting part about being fired and then getting a second chance is that you are no longer in a bargaining position. I had no leverage, so I swallowed my pride, said "thank you," and gladly took the jersey. It was like I was naked when I put it on. I felt like I was trying to play or coach left-handed. I felt lost. I had no connection to this number! Where was my identity going to come from? "I'm #15, not #28."

It wasn't until I started to turn my life around in the coming weeks, months, and years that I began to realize the significance of what was happening. It wasn't until I started living a life of *Faith + Action* that I truly began to put two and two together, and realize the path that God had started me down when He opened the door for me to get back in the game and put me in the only jersey left at UL... #28.

What He started that day was a message in my life, a story that would make it plain to see for everyone that something new is happening here. The message was that I was dead in the #15, but eventually I would be alive in Christ in the #28. Gone was the old me and in was the new me! Yes, He does make all things new, and He does take the broken and make them beautiful. I now had a new identity, and that identity was found in Christ. I was becoming a new creation. I was dying to my old, selfish ways, and was now beginning to live for Him.

As time went by and I became stronger and stronger in Christ, He began to fully open my eyes to see that He was doing something new. I began to see things that I had never seen before, things I would have missed had I been living a life of sin. He was showing me that He was now in control and that all I had to do was be me, take action, and live a life of faith. I began to see that the #28 was tied not to my identity, but to so many significant moments that God had orchestrated in my life to get me to this point. First of all, my name is Matthew and there are exactly 28 chapters in the book of Matthew in the Bible. Kathy and I were married on June 28, 1997 – the woman who, next to my relationship with the Lord, is the most important person in my life, yet also the one that I took for granted for so many years. Rob and I started our first day together at Texas A&M on the 28th day of June, 2005... an incredible journey for sure, full of the highest of highs and the lowest of lows, but it served to help shape the man I am today. I spent 28 days in rehab in the summer of 2010. Ugly, dark times for sure, but also a reminder that God can take those with scars and use them for His glory!

On October 28, 2011, I completed my training in New York, for Forest Pharmaceuticals, as a double-award winner. Yet another reminder of what I was capable of and what was to come if I would take action and walk by faith. Our house in College Station finally sold on April 28, 2012... further proof that we were on the right path. I quit drinking, for good, almost five years ago on February 28, 2013! How on earth was I to know I would quit drinking on the 28th day of February in 2013? I was still drinking when I went to UL. Like I've said many times, I can't make this stuff up. When I got the phone call informing me that they wanted to hire me here at Sam Houston State University, the date was June 28, 2014. Wait, it gets better! Kathy's devotional that morning, before I received the call, came out of ... you guessed it, Genesis 28:15! I get chills, even now while I'm writing this.

I am with you and will watch over you wherever you go, and I will bring you back to this land. I will not leave you until I have done what I have promised you.

~ Genesis 28:15

It's as if the verse out of Genesis 28:15 was God's way of speaking directly to us that day. It was God's way of saying, "Don't worry, I got this. Trust me and go." We had now come full circle, and God, after 2-1/2 amazing years, had brought us back to the land we had left, the Brazos Valley. Huntsville is only about 35-45 minutes from College Station, depending on who you get behind on Highway 30. We were coming home, back to Texas and back to the Houston area. We were coming back, but this time #15 wasn't coming. He was dead and gone; #28 was coming in his place, and he was coming back on a mission!

Pictured: This sign hangs above the door in our house that leads out to the garage. I read it every day before I leave. It reminds me that, "Every day is a gift" for me and my family. I am more determined than ever to never take a day for granted and to do my best to help and serve others along the way. The funny thing about this sign is that the first time I ever noticed it was in our house in Lafayette... When I told Kathy how much I loved the new sign and how much I loved seeing it every day, she informed me that it has been hanging in our home since we lived in College Station. I was blind, but now I see. Amen!

Epilogue

While I was finishing this book, we were grilling outside one night. Kyler was in the house and all three girls were outside with me as I was getting the steaks on the grill. Klaire, who is very inquisitive, looked up from her seat by the fire and asked out of the blue, "Daddy, if you could, would you go back and change anything that has happened throughout all of this?" Immediately I answered, "Yes, of course I would, sweetheart." To which she said, "What?" I then explained, "Well, I never would have started drinking again because I never meant to hurt you guys." I then turned the question back around on all three girls, "Is there anything y'all would go back and change?" With absolutely no hesitation whatsoever, they all answered in unison, "No." Surprised, I said, "Really? You guys wouldn't change anything?" Then they all three, in their own way, went on to explain to me that, no, they wouldn't. They shared that they loved the man I had become and who I was now. They were thankful for all the experiences that we have shared because they have helped them to grow in their faith. "Besides that," they said, "if we changed something, then we wouldn't be here, and we like it here." After that, I said, "Y'all good?" They said, "Yep." Then I told all three of them, "If y'all are good, then I'm good."

Kathy remains the love of my life and the "CEO" of our household. I couldn't ask for anything more in a wife, mother to my children, and best friend. I am so thankful that she has stuck by my side over all of these years.

Kyler is 18 years old and a senior in high school. He is extremely smart and driven. I look up to him in so many ways. He had to grow up faster than he should have, but it has only served to make him an incredibly strong and independent young man. He is currently working to get into MIT and study computer science.

Klaire is 14 years old and has become quite the volleyball player. She is a social butterfly who is very joyous and loves to laugh. Klaire has my sense of humor, so we understand and get each other's jokes, even when no one else does. Klaire is growing into an incredible young woman, with a very bright future.

Khloe, remains my little "Khlo-Khlo" even though she is twelve years old now and quickly growing into a beautiful young lady. She, like her older sister, loves volleyball. Kathy and I loved getting to watch her and Klaire play on the same team this year. Khloe is a "dog mom" at the tender age of 12 to "Bailey," an English Springer Spaniel, who I claim as my "grand-dog."

Me, I'm 46 years old now and finally living every day up to my true potential. Having found my calling, I really am a new man on a mission. God, family, friends, and career is how I prioritize my life now. I stay connected to the Lord and don't make a move without Him. I live now for my wife and kids, making time for those I love. I spend my days at work in a "construction zone," building men. I do a lot of speaking and absolutely love sharing God's story in my life as well as helping and mentoring other coaches and men. There is nothing I enjoy more than doing what I call "rolling up my sleeves" and getting dirty with others that may be hurt, broken, lost, or alone. Thank you, Jesus! I was dead, and now I'm alive!

The Five Lessons I Learned Along the Way

1. *There are (2) kinds of people: those that are humble and those that are about to be.* How you treat people matters. For years, I lived my life as an arrogant, egotistical jerk that really had no time for anyone, and made everything about myself. It wasn't until I lost everything that I realized that I had been such a jerk. I promised myself that if I ever made it back, I would treat everyone around me the way I wanted to be treated.

2. *Action:* I realized that if you want things to change, you have to do something about it. I was living a life of sin, and praying for God to save me at the same time. Guess what? God's not going to save you! Darkness does not and cannot live in the light. In fact, darkness by very definition does not exist. It's only an absence of light. I was in darkness. It wasn't until I stood up and took a single step that I realized God was with me the entire time and ready to take over from there. Are you hungry for God's blessings and miracles in your life? Then take ACTION!

3. *Respond:* The most important thing you will ever do in your life, when given the opportunity, is respond. Everyone gets knocked down. Everyone stumbles and falls, and you know what? That's not what people remember. They remember what you do about it. Adversity doesn't make you a man. It only reveals where you are as a man, and provides you the opportunity to roll over and give up or get back on your feet and press on.

4. _God rewards: Faith-Sacrifice-Obedience:_ Make no mistake, you will encounter trials of many kinds; but just as it says in the book of James, "Consider it pure joy when you encounter trials, because you know the testing of your faith develops perseverance and you need this to be mature and complete and lack nothing." I have found that by living a life of Faith, Sacrifice, and Obedience and at the same time having a grateful and thankful heart in any and all circumstances, that the Lord is eager to bless my work and the labor of my hands. I now bear good fruit in my life, in every area. Is it tough? Extremely! Are there hard days and trials? All the time, but is it worth it? Absolutely! I would rather live a life of Faith, Sacrifice, and Obedience in Christ and lose it all, than gain it all while living for myself.

5. _Love is undefeated:_ When you live, work, and play with a full heart, you win, no matter what the scoreboard says. If you do everything out of love, you have no fear. If you give fully of yourself, you don't need anything in return. There is a freedom, fearlessness, and humility that can only be obtained through love. Love really does conquer all.

FAITH + ACTION

One day while writing this book I received a phone call from the Texas City "Foundation for the Future." They were calling to inform me that they were going to be inducting me into the Texas City "Hall of Honor" in October of 2017. My initial reaction was, "Are they out of people to nominate in Texas City or what? How in the world, or better yet, why in the world would they choose me? There are so many more deserving people from Texas City that have done so much more with their lives." After the initial shock, it began to sink in. I thought, "I'm really going into the Texas City *Hall of Honor.* Unbelievable!"

It's amazing to see how far God has brought us on this journey – from living at my parents' house, drunk, unemployed, and having lost it all, to six years later seeing my family intact and thriving, and holding the head coaching position at Sam Houston State University. I've been sober for nearly five years, we've been blessed beyond our wildest dreams, and now being chosen to be in the Texas City *Hall of Honor.* On October 12, 2017, along with six other well-deserving nominees – one of them being none other than Jeff Banister, the manager of the Texas Rangers – I was inducted into the Texas City Hall of Honor.

Jesus looked at them and said, "With man this would be impossible, but with God, ALL things are possible."

~ Matthew 19:26

Pictured: Klaire, Kyler, me, Kathy, and Khloe, getting off the plane in Tallahassee in June of 2017. Our journey has been a wild one. We've seen the highest of the highs and have been to the lowest depths of the valley, but we are still here and are still standing. We are a stronger, more united family than ever before and are thankful for all our experiences.

Pictured: My Texas City High School "Hall of Honor" plaque. The plaque hangs in the main corridor of the high school, on the right when you walk in, and serves as further proof that FAITH + ACTION = ALL things are possible!

Thanks and Acknowledgments

I wrote this book in the hopes that it would serve in opening "the eyes" of the hearts of those who read it. My prayer is that my story would help save someone else that is lost or on the road to getting lost. This story is not, however, my story alone. There is a multitude of incredible people who have not only shared and lived this story, but have proven to be an inspiration for this story coming together. This book would not have been possible without the love, support, and help of the following people:

Kathy Deggs, Kyler Deggs, Klaire Deggs, Khloe Deggs, Gina Carr, Tyson Carr, Jimbo Deggs, Gaynell Deggs, Ernie Saldua, Jane Saldua, Minnie Hertenberger, Jeff Saldua, Abigail Saldua, Duke Austin, Earl Austin, Josh Foliart, Sean Matus, Donnie Higgs, Ernie Robles, Beau Mayne, Gary Miller, Jeremy Talbot, Dave Van Horn, Dave Jorn, Rob Childress, Anthony Babineaux, Tony Robichaux, Chris Domingue, Lance Harvell, Jay Sirianni, Shane Wedd, Lance Miles, Matt Morse, Dr. Hoyt, Bobby Williams, Pastor Nick Carroll, Ken Meyers, Sensei Micah, John Cohen, Chris Ballard, Kendall Rogers, along with all of the players that I learned so much from, friends that stuck by me, and the family that has always supported me.

Pictured: My sister and her family. L to R: Luke, Tyson, Gina, and Samuel Carr following our conference tournament championship in 2017. Although they live in North Carolina, they traveled to Texas for the tournament. Samuel was our "bat boy" the entire week. Gina took time away from her beautiful family to edit every word of this book. Thank you, "Geege." I love y'all.

My Favorite Bible Verses

Along this incredible journey, I have leaned heavily on God and the absolute Truth of His Living Word. I want to finish this book by leaving with you some of my favorite verses that have served to fill me up spiritually as well as help get me through some of the lowest valleys and darkest times. My prayer is that these verses lift you up the same way they did for me then and continue to do so today.

Genesis 28:15 "I am with you and will watch over you wherever you go, and I will bring you back to this land. I will not leave you until I have done what I have promised you."

Genesis 50:19-21 But Joseph said to them, "Don't be afraid. Am I in the place of God? You intended to harm me but God intended it for good to accomplish what is now being done, the saving of many lives. So then, don't be afraid. I will provide for you and your children." And he reassured them and spoke kindly to them.

Exodus 33:14 The Lord replied, "My presence will go with you, and I will give you rest."

Numbers 6:24-26 "The Lord bless you and keep you; The Lord make His face shine upon you and be gracious to you; The Lord turn his face toward you and give you peace."

Deuteronomy 6:5-6 Love The Lord your God with all your heart and with all your soul and with all of your strength. These commandments that I give you today are to be upon your hearts.

Deuteronomy 12:7 There in the presence of The Lord you God, you and your families shall eat & rejoice in everything you have put your hand to, because The Lord your God has blessed you.

Joshua 1:9   "Have I not commanded you? Be strong and courageous. Do not be afraid; do not be discouraged, for the Lord your God will be with you wherever you go."

Joshua 24:15   But if serving the Lord seems undesirable to you, then choose for yourselves this day whom you will serve, whether the gods your ancestors served beyond the Euphrates, or the gods of the Amorites, in whose land you are living. But as for me and my household, we will serve the Lord."

Judges 6:12   When the angel of the Lord appeared to Gideon, he said, "The Lord is with you, mighty warrior. "

1 Samuel 16:7   But the Lord said to Samuel, "Do not consider his appearance or his height, for I have rejected him. The Lord does not look at the things people look at. People look at the outward appearance, but the Lord looks at the heart."

1 Samuel 17:47   All those gathered here will know that it is not by sword or spear that the Lord saves; for the battle is the Lord's, and he will give all of you into our hands."

2 Chronicles 26:5   As long as he sought The Lord, God gave him success.

Nehemiah 8:10   "Do not grieve, for the joy of the Lord is your strength."

Job 1:21   "The Lord gave and the Lord has taken away; may the name of the Lord be praised."

Job 5:17   "Blessed is the one whom God corrects; so do not despise the discipline of the Almighty."

Job 6:13   "Do I have any power to help myself, now that success has been driven from me?"

Job 8:5-7 "But if you will seek God earnestly and plead with the Almighty, if you are pure and upright, even now he will rouse himself on your behalf and restore you to your prosperous state. Your beginnings will seem humble, so prosperous will your future be."

Job 9:10 He performs wonders that cannot be fathomed, miracles that cannot be counted.

Job 26:14 "Who then can understand the thunder of His Power?"

Job 36:21 Beware of turning to evil, which you seem to prefer to affliction.

Psalm 17:8 Keep me as the apple of your eye; hide me in the shadow of your wings.

Psalm 32:8 I will instruct you and teach you in the way you should go; I will counsel you with my loving eye on you.

Psalm 34:4 I sought the Lord, and he answered me; he delivered me from all my fears.

Psalm 34:18 The Lord is close to the brokenhearted and saves those who are crushed in spirit.

Psalm 34:22 The Lord redeems His servants…

Psalm 37:4-7 Take delight in the Lord, and he will give you the desires of your heart. Commit your way to the Lord; trust in him and he will do this: He will make your righteous reward shine like the dawn, your vindication like the noonday sun. Be still before the Lord and wait patiently for him…

Psalm 37:23 The Lord makes firm the steps of the one who delights in him; though he may stumble, he will not fall, for the Lord upholds him with his hand.

Psalm 40:1-3   I waited patiently for the Lord; he turned to me and heard my cry. He lifted me out of the slimy pit, out of the mud and mire; he set my feet on a rock and gave me a firm place to stand. He put a new song in my mouth, a hymn of praise to our God. Many will see and fear the Lord and put their trust in him.

Psalm 46:10   "Be still, and know that I am God… "

Psalm 51:10   Create in me a pure heart, O God, and renew a steadfast spirit within me.

Psalm 55:23   But as for me, I trust in You.

Psalm 90:17   May the favor of The Lord our God rest upon us; establish the work of our hands for us - yes, establish the work of our hands.

Psalm 91:14-15   "Because he loves me," says the Lord, "I will rescue him;
I will protect him, for he acknowledges my name. He will call on me, and I will answer him; I will be with him in trouble, I will deliver him and honor him.

Psalm 116:6   The Lord protects the simplehearted; when I was in great need He saved me.

Psalm 116:18   I will fulfill my vows to the Lord in the presence of all his people…

Psalm 118:17   I will not die but live, and will proclaim what The Lord has done.

Proverbs 2:6-8   For the Lord gives wisdom; from his mouth come knowledge and understanding. He holds success in store for the upright, he is a shield to those whose walk is blameless, for he guards the course of the just and protects the way of his faithful ones.

Proverbs 14:23 All hard work brings a profit, but mere talk leads only to poverty.

Proverbs 16:3 Commit to The Lord whatever you do, and your plans will succeed.

Proverbs 16:9 In his heart a man plans his course, but The Lord determines His steps.

Proverbs 16:26 The Laborer's appetite works for him; his hunger drives him on.

Proverbs 17:17 A friend loves at all times, and a brother is born for adversity.

Proverbs 22:1 A good name is more desirable than great riches; to be esteemed is better than silver or gold.

Proverbs 22:29 Do you see a man skilled in his work? He will serve before kings; he will not serve before obscure men.

Proverbs 27:17 As iron sharpens iron, so one man sharpens another.

Ecclesiastes 3:11 He has made everything beautiful in its time. He has also set eternity in the human heart; yet no one can fathom what God has done from beginning to end.

Ecclesiastes 5:19-20 Moreover, when God gives someone wealth and possessions, and the ability to enjoy them, to accept their lot and be happy in their toil – this is a gift of God. They seldom reflect on the days of their life, because God keeps them occupied with gladness of heart.

Isaiah 6:8 Then I heard the voice of the Lord saying, "Whom shall I send And who will go for us? " And I said, "Here am I. Send me!"

Isaiah 30:18 Yet the Lord longs to be gracious to you; therefore he will rise up to show you compassion. For the Lord is a God of justice. Blessed are all who wait for him!

Isaiah 30:21 Whether you turn to the right or to the left, your ears will hear a voice behind you, saying, "This is the way; walk in it."

Isaiah 40:31 ...but those who hope in the Lord will renew their strength. They will soar on wings like eagles; they will run and not grow weary, they will walk and not be faint.

Isaiah 41:13 For I am the Lord your God who takes hold of your right hand and says to you, Do not fear; I will help you.

Isaiah 43:1 "Fear not, for I have redeemed you; I have summoned you by name; you are mine."

Isaiah 43:18-19 "Forget the former things; do not dwell on the past. See, I am doing a new thing! Now it springs up; do you not perceive it? I am making a way in the wilderness and streams in the wasteland."

Isaiah 43:25 "I, even I, am he who blots out your transgressions, for my own sake, and remembers your sins no more."

Isaiah 55:8-9 For my thoughts are not your thoughts, neither are your ways my ways," declares the Lord. "As the heavens are higher than the earth, so are my ways higher than your ways and my thoughts than your thoughts."

Isaiah 55:11 The Lord will guide you always; he will satisfy your needs in a sun-scorched land and will strengthen your frame. You will be like a well-watered garden, like a spring whose waters never fail.

Jeremiah 17:7-8 "But blessed is the one who trusts in the Lord, whose confidence is in him. They will be like a tree planted by the water that sends out its roots by the stream. It does not fear when heat comes; its leaves are always green. It has no worries in a year of drought and never fails to bear fruit."

Jeremiah 29:11-14 For I know the plans I have for you," declares the Lord, "plans to prosper you and not to harm you, plans to give you hope and a future. Then you will call on me and come and pray to me, and I will listen to you. You will seek me and find me when you seek me with all your heart. I will be found by you," declares the Lord, "and will bring you back from captivity. I will gather you from all the nations and places where I have banished you," declares the Lord, "and will bring you back to the place from which I carried you into exile."

Joel 2:12-14 "Even now," declares the Lord, "return to me with all your heart, with fasting and weeping and mourning." Rend your heart and not your garments. Return to the Lord your God, for he is gracious and compassionate, slow to anger and abounding in love, and he relents from sending calamity. Who knows? He may turn and relent and leave behind a blessing —

Micah 7:7 But as for me, I watch in hope for the Lord, I wait for God my Savior; my God will hear me.

Zephaniah 3:15 The Lord has taken away your punishment, he has turned back your enemy.

Zephaniah 3:17 The Lord your God is with you, the Mighty Warrior who saves. He will take great delight in you; in his love he will no longer rebuke you, but will rejoice over you with singing."

Zephaniah 3:20 At that time I will gather you; at that time I will bring you home. I will give you honor and praise among all the peoples of the earth when I restore your fortunes before your very eyes," says the Lord.

Zechariah 3:7 "This is what the Lord Almighty says: 'If you will walk in obedience to me and keep my requirements, then you will govern my house and have charge of my courts, and I will give you a place among these standing here."

Zechariah 4:6 "Not by might nor by power, but by my Spirit," says the Lord Almighty.

Malachi 3:10 "Bring the whole tithe into the storehouse, that there may be food in my house. Test me in this," says the Lord Almighty, "and see if I will not throw open the floodgates of heaven and pour out so much blessing that there will not be room enough to store it."

Matthew 11:28 "Come to me, all you who are weary and burdened, and I will give you rest. Take my yoke upon you and learn from me, for I am gentle and humble in heart, and you will find rest for your souls. For my yoke is easy and my burden is light."

Matthew 19:26 Jesus looked at them and said, "With man this is impossible, but with God all things are possible."

Matthew 22:37-39 Jesus replied: "'Love the Lord your God with all your heart and with all your soul and with all your mind.' This is the first and greatest commandment. And the second is like it: 'Love your neighbor as yourself.'"

Mark 9:35 If anyone wants to be first, he must first be the very last, and servant of all.

Luke 5:31 Jesus answered them, "It is not the healthy who need a doctor, but the sick. I have not come to call the righteous, but sinners to repentance."

John 3:21 But whoever lives by the truth comes into the light, so that it may be seen plainly that what they have done has been done in the sight of God.

John 15:5 "I am the vine; you are the branches. If you remain in me and I in you, you will bear much fruit; apart from me you can do nothing."

John 15:13 Greater love has no one than this, that he lay down his life for his friends.

Romans 5:1 Therefore, since we have been justified through faith, we have peace with God through our Lord Jesus Christ...

Romans 8:28-30 And we know that in all things God works for the good of those who love him, who have been called according to his purpose. For those God foreknew he also predestined to be conformed to the image of his Son, that he might be the firstborn among many brothers and sisters. And those he predestined, he also called; those he called, he also justified; those he justified, he also glorified.

Romans 10:9-10 If you declare with your mouth, "Jesus is Lord," and believe in your heart that God raised him from the dead, you will be saved. For it is with your heart that you believe and are justified, and it is with your mouth that you profess your faith and are saved.

1 Corinthians 1:26-31 Brothers and sisters, think of what you were when you were called. Not many of you were wise by human standards; not many were influential; not many were of noble birth. But God chose the foolish things of the world to shame the wise; God chose the weak things of the world to shame the strong. God chose the lowly things of this world and the despised things – and the things that are not – to nullify the things that are, so that no one may boast before him. It is because of him that you are in Christ Jesus, who has become for us wisdom from God – that is, our righteousness, holiness and redemption. Therefore, as it is written: "Let the one who boasts boast in the Lord."

1 Corinthians 6:12 "I have the right to do anything," you say – but not everything is beneficial. "I have the right to do anything" – but I will not be mastered by anything.

1 Corinthians 10:13 No temptation has overtaken you except what is common to mankind. And God is faithful; he will not let you be tempted beyond what you can bear. But when you are tempted, he will also provide a way out so that you can endure it.

1 Corinthians 15:57 But thanks be to God! He gives us the victory through our Lord Jesus Christ.

1 Corinthians 16:13 Be on your guard; stand firm in the faith; be courageous; be strong. Do everything in love.

2 Corinthians 5:17 Therefore, if anyone is in Christ, the new creation has come: The old has gone, the new is here!

2 Corinthians 12:8-10 Three times I pleaded with the Lord to take it away from me. But he said to me, "My grace is sufficient for you, for my power is made perfect in weakness. " Therefore I will boast all the more gladly about my weaknesses, so that Christ's power may rest on me. That is why, for Christ's sake, I delight in weaknesses, in insults, in hardships, in persecutions, in difficulties. For when I am weak, then I am strong.

Galatians 5:1 It is for freedom that Christ has set us free. Stand firm, then, and do not let yourselves be burdened again by a yoke of slavery.

Galatians 6:9 Let us not become weary in doing good, for at the proper time we will reap a harvest if we do not give up.

Ephesians 2:8-9 For it is by grace you have been saved, through faith – and this is not from yourselves, it is the gift of God – not by works, so that no one can boast.

Ephesians 3:20 Now to him who is able to do immeasurably more than all we ask or imagine, according to his power that is at work within us…

Ephesians 5:20 … always giving thanks to God the Father for everything, in the name of our Lord Jesus Christ.

Philippians 2:3-5 Do nothing out of selfish ambition or vain conceit. Rather, in humility value others above yourselves, not looking to your own interests but each of you to the interests of the others.

In your relationships with one another, have the same mindset as Christ Jesus…

Philippians 3:8 What is more, I consider everything a loss because of the surpassing worth of knowing Christ Jesus my Lord, for whose sake I have lost all things.

Philippians 3:13-14 Brothers and sisters, I do not consider myself yet to have taken hold of it. But one thing I do: Forgetting what is behind and straining toward what is ahead, I press on toward the goal to win the prize for which God has called me heavenward in Christ Jesus.

Philippians 3:18-20 For, as I have often told you before and now tell you again even with tears, many live as enemies of the cross of Christ. Their destiny is destruction, their god is their stomach, and their glory is in their shame. Their mind is set on earthly things. But our citizenship is in heaven. And we eagerly await a Savior from there, the Lord Jesus Christ…

Philippians 4:11-13 … for I have learned to be content whatever the circumstances. I know what it is to be in need, and I know what it is to have plenty. I have learned the secret of being content in any and every situation, whether well fed or hungry, whether living in plenty or in want. I can do all this through him who gives me strength.

Colossians 3:23 Whatever you do, work at it with all your heart, as working for the Lord, not for human masters…

1 Thessalonians 5:16-17   Rejoice always, pray continually, give thanks in all circumstances; for this is God's will for you in Christ Jesus.

1 Timothy 2:3   Endure hardship with us like a good soldier of Christ Jesus.

2 Timothy 1:7   For the Spirit God gave us does not make us timid, but gives us power, love and self-discipline.

1 Timothy 3:16   All Scripture is God-breathed and is useful for teaching, rebuking, correcting and training in righteousness, so that the servant of God may be thoroughly equipped for every good work.

Hebrews 10:35-36   So do not throw away your confidence; it will be richly rewarded. You need to persevere so that when you have done the will of God, you will receive what he has promised.

Hebrews 10:39   But we do not belong to those who shrink back and are destroyed, but to those who have faith and are saved.

Hebrews 11:1   Now faith is confidence in what we hope for and assurance about what we do not see.
Hebrews 11:6   And without faith it is impossible to please God, because anyone who comes to him must believe that he exists and that he rewards those who earnestly seek him.

Hebrews 12:2-3   fixing our eyes on Jesus, the pioneer and perfecter of faith. For the joy set before him he endured the cross, scorning its shame, and sat down at the right hand of the throne of God. Consider him who endured such opposition from sinners, so that you will not grow weary and lose heart.

Hebrews 12:7   Endure hardship as discipline; God is treating you as his children. For what children are not disciplined by their father?

James 1:2-4   Consider it pure joy, my brothers and sisters, whenever you face trials of many kinds, because you know that the testing of your faith produces perseverance. Let perseverance finish its work so that you may be mature and complete, not lacking anything.

James 4:6   "God opposes the proud but gives grace to the humble."

James 4:7-8   Submit yourselves, then, to God. Resist the devil, and he will flee from you. Come near to God and he will come near to you.

1 Peter 1:13-14   Therefore, with minds that are alert and fully sober, set your hope on the grace to be brought to you when Jesus Christ is revealed at his coming.

1 Peter 4:10   Each of you should use whatever gift you have received to serve others, as faithful stewards of God's grace in its various forms.

1 Peter 5:6-7   Humble yourselves, therefore, under God's mighty hand, that he may lift you up in due time. Cast all your anxiety on him because he cares for you.

1 Peter 5:10-11   And the God of all grace, who called you to his eternal glory in Christ, after you have suffered a little while, will himself restore you and make you strong, firm and steadfast. To him be the power for ever and ever. Amen.

1 John 1:5   God is light; in him there is no darkness at all.

1 John 2:15-17   Do not love the world or anything in the world. If anyone loves the world, love for the Father is not in them. For everything in the world – the lust of the flesh, the lust of the eyes, and the pride of life – comes not from the Father but from the world. The world and its desires pass away, but whoever does the will of God lives forever.

1 John 3:18 Dear children, let us not love with words or speech but with actions and in truth.

1 John 7-11 Dear friends, let us love one another, for love comes from God. Everyone who loves has been born of God and knows God. Whoever does not love does not know God, because God is love. This is how God showed his love among us: He sent his one and only Son into the world that we might live through him. This is love: not that we loved God, but that he loved us and sent his Son as an atoning sacrifice for our sins. Dear friends, since God so loved us, we also ought to love one another. No one has ever seen God; but if we love one another, God lives in us and his love is made complete in us.

Revelation 3:7-8 What he opens no one can shut, and what he shuts no one can open. I know your deeds. See, I have placed before you an open door that no one can shut. I know that you have little strength, yet you have kept my word and have not denied my name.

Revelation 3:19-22 "Those whom I love I rebuke and discipline. So be earnest and repent. Here I am! I stand at the door and knock. If anyone hears my voice and opens the door, I will come in and eat with that person, and they with me.

To the one who is victorious, I will give the right to sit with me on my throne, just as I was victorious and sat down with my Father on his throne. Whoever has ears, let them hear what the Spirit says to the churches."

About The Author

Matt Deggs is the Head Baseball Coach at Sam Houston State University in Huntsville, Texas. He is beginning his 23rd year as a college baseball coach, with close to 18 of those years coming at the NCAA D-1 level.

In addition to serving as the head baseball coach at Sam Houston State University, Deggs has had coaching stints at: The University of Louisiana at Lafayette (Ragin' Cajuns), Texas A&M, The University of Arkansas, Texarkana Junior College, & Northwestern State University.

Deggs, who for years was a transactional coach that only lived for himself, was addicted to alcohol and consequently destroyed a career, family and countless relationships along the way. He now is a changed man.

Going from bearing bad fruit or little to no fruit at all, Deggs has seen his life come full circle and now strives to live a life full of service, impact, development and bearing good fruit not only in his life but in the lives of his family, friends and players.

Deggs by the grace of God has been married to his wife Kathy for 20 years. They have 3 children: Kyler (18), Klaire (14) & Khloe (12)... They reside in Huntsville, Texas.

Coaching is only part of what Deggs does now. He also speaks to churches, groups, companies and other men & coaches... not only of his journey and testimony, but also in the fields of leadership, team building & transformational coaching.

Deggs has been to the highest of highs and the lowest lows and has found a way to climb all the way back... his life has been one of blessing, tragedy and triumph; a life of defying odds and battling back.

The Pack Video System

Throughout this online video program, you will uncover the foundation of what has helped Coach Deggs' lead record-breaking teams.

The Pack Video System includes **nearly 3 hours** of Coach Deggs' teaching his proven formula to building teams with strong identity, clear purpose, and unbreakable culture.

Visit
CoachDeggs.com
to learn more and get started today!

Speaking

Coach Deggs delivers **keynote and transformational speaking engagements** to leaders, athletic teams, churches, and corporate organizations across the country.

Visit

CoachDeggs.com

to book Coach Deggs to speak at your next event!

71714996R00141

Made in the USA
San Bernardino, CA
19 March 2018